THE BICHON FRISE

Lexiann Grant

The Bichon Frise
An Interpet Book

Project Team
Editor: Heather Russell-Revesz
Copy Editor: Joann Woy
Design: Angela Stanford
Series Design: Mada Design and Stephanie Krautheim
Series Originator: Dominique De Vito

First published in UK by
Interpet Publishing
Vincent Lane
Dorking
Surrey
RH4 3YX

ISBN 13 978-1-84286-151-6

This book has been published with the intent to provide accurate and authoritative information in regard to the subject matter within. While every precaution has been taken in preparation of this book, the author and publisher expressly disclaim responsibility for any errors, omissions, or adverse effects arising from the use or application of the information contained herein. The techniques and suggestions are used at the reader's discretion and are not to be considered a substitute for veterinary care. If you suspect a medical problem consult your veterinarian.

Interpet Publishing

TABLE OF CONTENTS

HISTORY

of the Bichon Frise

Little white dogs have been a part of our history for at least 2,000 years. Ancient artwork from Greece and Rome, and the writings of Pliny the Elder (d. 79 C.E.) record the presence of these dogs in the lives of merchants, noblemen, and sea traders.

Although true breed types as we recognise them today were not defined as such until the Victorian era, dogs who were the forerunners of the Bichon Frise have been around for many centuries. The breed's history, like that of most breeds, derives from legends passed down over the years, combined with bits of history pieced together to forge the story of the Bichon Frise.

THE "TAIL" OF THE BICHON FRISE

The route the Bichon breed took from antiquity to the present began with the Phoenician traders. These seafaring people are believed to have carried little white dogs with them, as goods to be traded for other products along their routes.

One of the main ports of call for the Bichon Frise was Tenerife, the largest of the Canary Islands, located off the northwest coast of Africa. From here, the dogs were later rediscovered by either Italian or Spanish sailors, who brought them back to Europe where they become favourites of the nobility.

The Bichon Frise, known then as the "Tenerife Bichon," "Tenerife Terrier," or "Barbichon," is reported to have been introduced to the French court by King François I (reign 1494–1547), then popularised by King Henri III (reign 1574–1589). During this same period, the little dogs are reported to also have been found in the Spanish and Italian courts. Art from the Renaissance era portrays many such small, white dogs, some with curly coats.

For the next 200 to 300 years, the Bichon enjoyed a pampered life among the upper classes of European society, but eventually the dog fell from his high position and became a dog of the streets.

Dogs who were the forerunners of the Bichon Frise have been around for many centuries.

Bichons had to earn their living as working dogs, helping organ grinders and circus acts entertain crowds.

By the mid-1900s the little white dogs were struggling to survive, until their popularity was restored after the World Wars, and the breed became firmly established as one of today's foremost companion dogs.

SPANNING THE CENTURIES

It may be possible to fill in some of the blanks about the Bichon's development by looking at the history surrounding this breed's journey from the past to the present, beginning with the Phoenicians.

In Antiquity

According to the *Encyclopedia Phoenicia*, ancient authorities did not recount information about Phoenician trade in the Fortunate Islands (today's Canary Islands). It is surmised that the islands were used as a supply stop en route to destinations around the coast of Africa. It is also noted that, because of fear of the island's natives, except for capturing some of the large, wild dogs, no trade was conducted.

Plinius, a Roman naturalist, records that some of these mastiff-type dogs were given to King Jubal, vassal ruler of Roman-conquered Mauritania (present day Morocco), sometime between 25 and 19 B.C.E. Jubal then renamed these nearby islands "Canarias," from the Latin word *canis*, meaning dog, after the wild dogs which inhabited the islands.

Despite the incompleteness of historical documentation, a few, scant records describe a small, whitish dog with a long, silky coat on an island frequented by the Phoenicians in the Mediterranean between Italy and Africa. This island, which would later be known as Malta, is believed to be the location of origin of the Maltese dog.

The Phoenicians are also credited with the spread of a slightly larger, similar dog with a coat of white and varied shades, from islands off the eastern coast of Africa. Later named the Coton de Tulear during French colonisation, these dogs come from Reunion and Madagascar. Today, the "Bichon" of this region is officially recognised as the royal dog of Madagascar. Like the Phoenicians, French trade would later carry this dog around the world to more exotic regions.

With the fall of the Roman Empire (150–475 B.C.E.) and the cessation of Phoenician trade in the early 600s, the transportation of small white dogs around the Mediterranean Basin is also likely to have ground to a halt. For several centuries, Bichon-type dogs who may have regularly traveled throughout southern and western Europe and northern Africa and its coastal islands would have become isolated, allowing the possibility of type definition to evolve.

German cynologist S. Duhel believed that barbarian hordes, such as the Vandals, may have taken medium-sized, whitish, spitz-like dogs into southern Europe—including through the Iberian peninsula—during this time. It is possible that these dogs may have influenced the development of the Bichon.

On the Iberian Peninsula

Little mention is made of the Canary Islands again until 1336, when European map makers record their name and location. By this

It is possible that spitz-like dogs may have influenced the development of the Bichon.

Little white dogs were popular in the French court of Henri III.

time, sturdy-boned, curly-coated spaniels could be readily found working the waters of western Europe, including France and Spain.

Supported by Prince Henrique the Navigator, during the early 1400s, Portugal sent several expeditions to Africa and nearby islands, including the Canaries. Later in the same century, Vasco de Gama, a Portuguese explorer, described the dogs of the Canary Islands, writing, "Their numerous dogs resemble those of Portugal, and bark like them."

Portuguese dogs at that time historically included large flock guardians, heavily built mastiff-type estate guardians, Greyhound-like sight-hounds, and water spaniels. More diverse types may have existed, including the Bichons, but they are not described in writings of the period, either on the Canary Islands or in Portugal.

However, it is not unreasonable to presume that Portuguese explorers may have played a role in bringing the foundation stock for the Bichon to the attention of the European continent. Additionally, small white lap dogs who are possible forerunners of the Bichon are seen in Portuguese portraiture from this time.

In 1480, Portugal ceded the Canary Islands to Spain, and Spanish control of trade from the Canaries and other islands began. In a few decades, dogs who resemble today's Bichon Frise and some slightly larger, like the Spanish Water Dog (SWD), can be found portrayed in Spanish art of the period, and countries who traded with Spain began to illustrate similar lap dogs in their art.

Spanish Water Dogs

Although this history doesn't begin to provide all the missing links in the Bichon's development, a glimpse at the SWD may give a hint of another possible contributor to the breed's origin. The SWD is a moderate dog in size and structure, with a curly coat of several medium and light shades, but with a preponderance of solid white coats.

Water spaniels were an established type of working dog during this era, and would have been taken on many sea journeys to aid with shipboard tasks and in providing food. Smaller dogs would have required fewer supplies on longer journeys, so it is conceivable that sailors opted for a smaller dog than the SWD, and chose a dog who may have more closely resembled the Bichon.

A Renaissance Fashion

Along with the Renaissance and its explosion of art, culture, and science, came many European wars. France invaded Italy, Spain occupied Flanders (a portion of Belgium), and England engaged in power struggles with Spain for control of sea trade. With these tides of war and cultural change came little white dogs.

Many of these dogs had silky coats, some had wavy coats or tight curls, a few were medium boned while others had petite frames. It is not possible to determine the exact breed of each, although they variously resembled the Bolognese, Maltese, small Poodle, and the Bichon.

Accounts describe French King Henri III and his court carrying their favoured white dogs in boxes around their necks, in pockets, and inside garment sleeves. While legend has it that these dogs were Bichons, other histories recount these dogs as possibly being Poodles or Maltese.

One point remains clear: from the frequency of their appearance in portraits of the royal and noble households, these little white dogs—many of whom distinctly look like Bichons—were extremely popular.

A Dog's Job

While history clearly records the inclusion of dogs on board ships during the age of exploration, it should be kept in mind that these dogs would be required to earn their keep in some manner. Because of the limitation of food and fresh water rations, no dogs would have been taken who could not provide a service in return. These duties would have included hunting and killing rats, retrieving fish or water tools, providing warmth to sailors, and the supposed "bearing away" of fleas from the ship's crew members.

It should also be remembered that even the small lap dogs owned and pampered by the upper classes in the ensuing centuries would still have been required to perform a function. Companion dogs served as fashion statements, declarations of wealth, provided warmth during chilly outings and cold nights to their owners, and were thought to remove fleas from their owner's bedding and bodies.

Barbichon

The word *barbichon* is applied to the group of small, long-haired white lap dogs that have beards and curls.

As trade and war brought wealth to western and Mediterranean European countries, clothing and hairstyles become more elaborate. Haute couture dictated that every garment should be intricately embellished. Lace, embroidery, ruffles, ribbons, and curly hair were all the fashion. This applied to dogs as well, and thus a movement toward selecting the more curly-coated small white dogs may have consciously begun.

As fashions became more ornate, those who dressed in fine style were known as "dandies." Etymology does not delineate which designation came first—the excessively fashionable people

After the French revolution, Bichons were often found at the sides of street performers.

or the dogs—but this trend did result in a new word, *bichonner*: to dandify, beribbon, or pamper. This word was modified to apply specifically to the group of popular, small, long-haired white lap dogs sporting beards and curls: *barbichon*.

The Tides Turn

On the opposite side of the street was a class of society that was as depressed and poor as the upper classes were wealthy and extravagant. As starvation, disease, and poverty increased, and dissatisfaction with the perceived moral corruption of the nobility grew, religious and political movements arose that attempted to stifle lavish displays of wealth. In France, peasants and commoners revolted to overthrow the ruling class.

The Bichons, seen as symbols of their owners' elitist attitudes, were deposed as well. Although the types are not specifically described, records exist showing that when a nobleman's family was sent to jail, their dogs went with them. Other nobles who fled capture abandoned their lap dogs to fend for themselves in the streets.

Their athleticism and natural inclination to entertain helped the small white dogs to adapt to life on the street. By entertaining street performers and onlookers with their dancing antics, the dogs were able to beg food and shelter, eventually earning a place in the performers' regular repertoires.

While the Bichon may have been a participant in the larger circus troupes, the preferred dogs there were Poodles. The Bichon's newfound spot in the streets placed him most frequently in the company of organ grinders and gypsy caravans. Present-day owners must wonder if the Bichon's larcenous tendencies may have been another talent that his gypsy owners utilised to pick the pockets of the people in the crowds.

The popularity of Bichons temporarily flourished around the end of the nineteenth century on the continent during the Belle Epoch—when society strove to surround themselves with grace and beauty—but this period was short lived. During much of the Victorian era, the middle and upper classes in England and the United States developed a rigid sense of social order and standardised goals of perfection, which were applied to animals (including dogs) as well. Because of the Bichon's association with the "less desirable elements" of society, and because of the

Celebrity Bichon Owners

Many celebrities have enjoyed the adorable Bichon, including Eve Arden, John Forsyth, Kathy Lee Gifford, Susan Lucci, Candy Spelling (wife of producer Aaron Spelling), Barbara Streisand, Barbara Bradford Taylor, and Betty White.

unkempt appearance of their coat, the Bichon once more fell into disrepute.

Although still surviving as an entertainer of the streets, the two World Wars nearly wiped out the plucky little white dogs. The destruction, and food and supply shortages of the wars resulted in the near loss of many breeds of dogs. During World War II, gypsies were among the peoples sent to Nazi concentration camps. Their performing Bichons also fell victim to this campaign, and the breed faded into near extinction.

Fédération Cynologique Internationale

The Fédération Cynologique Internationale is the World Canine Organization, which includes 80 members and contract partners (one member per country), each of which issues its own pedigrees and trains its own judges. The founding nations were Germany, Austria, Belgium, France, and the Netherlands. It was first formed in 1911, but later disappeared during World War I. The organisation was reconstituted in 1921. Currently, neither the United States nor Canada is a member.

The FCI ensures that its pedigrees and judges are recognised by all FCI members. Every member country conducts international shows as well as working trials; results are sent to the FCI office, where they are input into computers. When a dog has been awarded a certain number of awards, he can receive the title of International Beauty or Working Champion. These titles are confirmed by the FCI.
The FCI recognises 331 dog breeds, and each of them is the "property" of a specific country, ideally the one in which the breed developed. The owner countries of the breeds write the standard of these breeds in cooperation with the Standards and Scientific Commissions of the FCI, and the translation and updating are carried out by the FCI.

In addition, via the national canine organisation and the FCI, every breeder can ask for international protection of his or her kennel name.

BICHONS IN FRANCE

Following the devastation of Europe after World War I, the Bichon as a breed barely survived. In France, a few enthusiasts assembled the dogs they could find and made a concerted effort to restore the breed. A few notable kennels established lines and breeding programmes designed to follow type.

The first official breed standard was drafted in conjunction with The Friends of Belgian Breeds, by Madame Abadie of Stern Vor kennels and refined by Madame Bouctovagniez, President of the Toy Club of France. Since the white curly dogs were still being referred to by multiple names, the President of the Fédération Cynologique Internationale (FCI), Madame Nizet de Leemans, proposed that the breed be designated as the "Bichon à poil Frisé."

With a name and description uniquely their own, the Bichon Frise standard was adopted on March 5, 1933, by the Société Centrale Canine de France and admitted to the kennel club's stud book roles on October 18, 1934. The FCI noted the Bichon as a French-Belgian breed with the right to register dogs in their "Book of Origins" from all countries. However, early after its acceptance, the Bichon was only recognised by the kennel clubs of France, Belgium, and Italy.

The Bichons who remained in Europe after World War II were once again used to rebuild the breed and, particularly in France, their popularity rose again and stablised.

BICHONS IN THE UK

Given the proximity of France and England, it would be logical to think that the Bichon Frise would arrive on British shores before making it over the Atlantic to North America. However, we have the USA to thank for bringing the Bichon to Britain!

Bichons were brought back to the United States with returning service personnel after World War I, but no kennels or breeding programmes were established, and the breed did not catch on.

It wasn't until 1956 that the Bichon gained a foothold in the USA when Mr and Mrs Fracois Piqcault emigrated to Wisconsin with their dogs, including a breeding pair from the Stern Vor kennel, based in France. A litter was born out of Étoile de Stern Vor by Eddie White de Stern Vor. It took the dedicated work of a number of leading American breeders to promote the breed and to establish the Bichon Frise Club of America, which was founded in 1964. The aim was to achieve official recognition by the American Kennel Club, and this was awarded in 1973.

Natural Charms

Despite the Bichon's rapid progress towards AKC recognition, the dogs were not well accepted in the show ring at first. In Europe, Bichons were shown with a natural coat, but in the United States this ungroomed look was considered messy and unappealing.

It wasn't until the 1950s that the Bichon became popular in the United States.

Bichon Frise Club of Great Britain

The Bichon Frise Club of Great Britain exists to safeguard and promote the Bichon Frise. Their goals and objectives include:

• To render assistance to breeders and owners

• To encourage and assist in the breeding of sound and healthy Bichon Frise, free from abnormalities and conforming to the Kennel Club standard for the Bichon Frise.

See Appendix for full Bichon Frise breed standard.

Frank Sabella, then a handler who later became a respected AKC judge, made a presentation to the BFCA on how to groom the Bichon into a fluff of appealing, clean fur. In the next few years, a strong push was made to present Bichons in this formal trim, and the breed began to rise in ring popularity. This look, with slight modification to the shape of the cut on the head, beard, and ears, is the look still seen at shows today.

First Arrivals

There was growing interest in the new breed, recently launched in America, but Britain had no breeding stock to draw on until Mr and Mrs Sorstein from the USA came to live in England in 1973. They brought with them a pair of American-bred Bichons: Rava's Regal Valor of Reenroy and Jenny Vivre de Carlisle. The 'Carlisle' Bichons, belonging to the Sorsteins, can be found in the background of most of the original Bichons born in the UK. By great good luck, a pet Bichon had been registered by the Kennel Club in 1957, and this very early registration meant that the breed was eligible for KC registration as soon as the first Bichons arrived from America.

The Bichon made its show debut in Britain in 1974 at the Hammersmith Open Show. The new breed was an instant success. The puppy Carlise Cicero of Tresilva won Best Rare Breed, Best Puppy in Show, and Reserve Best in Show. The Bichon Frise had arrived in style! The breed was soon strengthened with the arrival of more American-bred dogs, including a number of bitches in whelp. They were imported by John and Wendy Streatfield of the Leander kennel.

Official Recognition

Moves were made to form a breed club in 1974, and the founding members were a distinguished bunch made up of leading breeders and judges. A number of exhibitors from those early days went on to be highly influential in the breed. They included Vera Goold (Leijazulip), Paddy Holbrook O'Hara (Appleacres), Ivy Colvin and her daughter Anthea Marsh (Vythea), and Jackie Ransom (Tresilva). Despite many applications, it was not until 1977 that the Bichon Frise Club of Great Britain received official Kennel Club recognition, and was entitled to hold its own shows.

The first Open Show was held in January 1978, and Best in Show went to Wendy Streafield's import, Am. Ch. Vogelflights Choir Boy Of Leander. In 1981 Challenge Certificates were awarded for the first time.

Top Bichon

In 2001, Am. Ch. Special Times Just Right (JR) won America's top award, going Best in Show at the prestigious Westminster Kennel Club show.

KISSING COUSINS

Today's small, white companion dogs of all types may share similar origins. One theory is that spitz-like dogs from the north were transported into the Mediterranean basin, possibly through Roman conquests and later with attacking tribes, and were developed into the small, white companion dogs of old.

Another theory proposes that these dogs were developed by crossing toy spaniels and Miniature Poodles, while a similar theory suggests that crosses were made between water spaniels or Poodles and the Maltese. A more traditional theory believes the Bichon to be derived from the Barbet, a large, French water spaniel, through crosses to the prominent, small white lap dogs, from which the name *Barbichon* is thought to derive.

While these crosses may have resulted in Bichon-type dogs, breeding for specific type did not exist until the late nineteenth century, and the knowledge of such breeding techniques likely would not have been utilised at the time the Bichon appeared. By the middle of the sixteenth century, noblemen did keep dogs who performed various types of work, but these dogs were known only by their functions, not as individually named breeds.

Additionally, the Maltese- and Poodle-type dogs came on the scene at about the same time as the Bichon, so are probably not prominent

Today's small white companion dogs of all types may share similar origins.

progenitors of the breed. While the Barbet is older, the existence of medium and small curly-coated white dogs in the Iberian peninsula coincides with the existence of the Barbet. And the dogs of France (from where the Bichons are presumed to have sprung) during this period historically included stylish scent hounds named by estate or description; griffons and bassets, which were named for their wiry hair or short legs; or the vendeens, which were slow-moving hunting dogs.

Cynologists who focus on the developmental history of dog types have noted that the Bichons and the Lowchen, or lion dogs, were likely a product of breedings that naturally occurred in the oceanic lands near ports of call for world trade routes. (Note:

Lowchen breeders today dispute this theory and believe their breed to be descended from Tibetan dogs. This is an interesting possibility, since a far-east Asian theory of origin exists for the water dogs who are believed to be ancestors of the Bichons.)

The migratory transportation of dogs throughout the region and time makes it impossible to determine precisely how, when, and where the Bichon Frise came into being. Despite the lack of documentation, history supports that the Bichon was a seafarer, and is related to or descended from ancient water dogs surrounding the trade routes.

The group of Barbichons, or small white dogs who served as companions for centuries, include not only the Bichon a poil Frise, but also the Bichon Maltaise, the Bichon Bolognese, the Bichon Havanese, the Coton de Tulear, and possibly the Lowchen as well. These "cousins" are believed to have originated in, respectively: Malta, an island near Italy and north Africa; Bologna, Italy; Havana, Cuba; Madagascar, an island off the east coast of Africa; and Holland and Germany.

Notable Names, Past & Present

There have been a number of outstanding Bichons in Britain who have made a remarkable contribution to the breed.

- From the total entry of 77 dogs entered at the first Open Show, eight were sired by Aust. Ch. Jazz de la Butherie of Leijazulip, a dog who really made his mark on the breed.
- The breed's first recordholder was Ch. Ir. Ch. Tiopepi Mad Louie of Pamplona who was the top winning Bichon for three years, and won the Toy Group at Crufts in 1987.
- Ch. Sibon Fatal Attraction at Pamplona, a phenomenal winner with some 32 Challenge Certificates, 22 Group wins, and Top Dog All Breeds in 1990.
- Ch. Warmingham Scarlet O'Hara, a breed recordholder, who was later overtaken by Ch. Roxara He Drives You Wild.

In most recent times, the top winning dog has been an American import, Ch. & Am Ch. Paray's I Told You So, who looks set to become the next breed recordholder.

There are a number of highly successful Bichon kennels in the UK, currently producing top quality dogs, including Bobander, Rushmar, Sulyka and Warmingham.

Despite their close origins, the Bichon Frise is the only curly, double-coated dog in this group. These differences provoke questions about the foundation of the breed which may never be answered.

Whatever the breed's history, one thing is certain about the Bichon: He was—and is—one of the most beloved companion dogs throughout the world for many centuries and for years to come.

2

CHARACTERISTICS

of the Bichon Frise

There's no doubt about how enchanting the Bichon Frise is. Just one look and most dog lovers are smitten by the breed's engaging smile, and they can't wait to get their hands into the fluffy white fur that begs to be touched. But how does such a near perfect breed come about? Through breeders who have clearly defined in writing how the Bichon should look and act, and who then follow the guidelines of this description when choosing which sire and dam to breed for puppies.

This written guideline is known as a *breed standard*. The standard is the blueprint for building Bichons who will always look and act like Bichons. Without this standard to guide breeders over the years, the Bichon appearance could drift away from the type of dog recognised today.

BUILDING A BICHON FRISE

The description of the Bichon Frise begins with what the dog should look like in general: In a word—fluffy. Despite its technical language elsewhere, the standard notes that the dog should look like a white powder puff and act like a happy, upbeat, extrovert exuding self-confidence. Attention is paid to the expression, or how the Bichon's face should show these positive attitudes.

The standard also describes a dog who should be well balanced. The Bichon should be seen as a real dog—not a tiny replica or a stuffed toy—a dog who has no one physical characteristic emphasised above all else.

Weights, Measures, and Build

When building anything—even a dog—the builder, or breeder in this case, must work with predetermined sizes and dimensions. In the Bichon, the structure is well-proportioned and well-balanced. Bichon height should run between 9 and 11 inches (23 and 28 cm) and range no more than 2 inches (5 cm). Although the standard does not define a weight range, Bichons usually weigh between 12 and 15 pounds (5 and 9 kg), but this can vary depending on height and build.

Standards to Breed By

The dictionary defines "standard" as a model, approved by an authority source, which is used as a foundation against which other representations are compared. This is true when applied to the breed standards for all pedigree dogs.

These standards are prepared by people with a long history and experience in their breed, and the documents describe what the perfect specimen of that dog should be. This description covers structure, movement, type, and temperament. Because no dog is perfect, the standard is used as a template for breeding and judging the ideal dog, and for producing future generations of healthy, happy companion animals.

Despite his diminutive height, the Bichon is a dog of substance, who should be well muscled. His frame should be medium-boned, although a slight trend toward finer bones has been seen with the increase in popularity of the breed. The Bichon should never be perceived as a dog who is frail or delicate.

Heads Up

Much of the standard's emphasis is placed on the Bichon head, face, and expression. A large part of the Bichon charm is his round black eyes, enhanced with black eyelids and rims, peering out of a bright, white face. The button black nose, in a triangle with the eyes, completes the picture of a happy dog.

Since the expressive face is such a key feature of the Bichon, it is vital to the breed's appearance that light or pale eyes or pigment of the facial leather be strictly avoided. The lips are likewise black, another key element in the winning Bichon smile.

To get that picture-perfect Bichon face, the head must be properly shaped. The head should be of sufficient size and proportion so that the eyes can be round and expressively opened wide, but without excess.

The nose is distinct from the forehead and adds emphasis to the roundness of the overall head. Ears are floppy and flowing, but shouldn't be so long as to hide the eyes or distract from the pleasing balance of the well-defined muzzle. Although the ears are dropped, they should be set to enhance the engaged, alert look of the Bichon face.

All Connected

To carry it all off, the Bichon must have just the right neck and body shape. The neck plays the supporting role when it comes to Bichon attitude. It is arched and fairly long, so that when the dog moves, the head is held up, not forward. This lends the appearance of a proud carriage, attentiveness, and a lively personality.

The body should be gracefully curved, yet substantial. The chest should be well-formed, allowing for plenty of movement, and rib cage is slightly rounded. When observing a nicely shaped Bichon, the impression is one of gently flowing roundness.

Topping off this picture is the plumy tail. When set into the body at just the right level with the back, the Bichon tail should curve up and around in a stylish plume of fur. The tail makes a proud statement about the dog's jaunty, friendly nature.

Much of the breed standard's emphasis is placed on the Bichon's head, face, and expression.

Coming and Going

At one time, the Bichon had shorter legs that tended to bow in the front, often with front feet that turned outwards. Today's Bichon has a slightly longer leg, more in proportion to the body. Legs have also straightened, but with correct angles and, when set into the shoulders properly, allow movement that is not stiff legged.

To maintain proportion, the rear legs should be angled in the same manner. Hips and thighs should look muscular, as would be found in a canine athlete. Paws should be round to fit with the rest of the Bichon shape and, like the dark pigment of the face, foot pads should be black.

The Bichon should present as beautiful a picture in motion as he does in repose. A smooth effortless trot is the preferred gait. Legs move in balance and, regardless of the direction from which you view a moving Bichon, the motion should be equally distributed. Pads on the feet should be visible while moving and the head and neck remain up. A Bichon on the go should move with a free-flowing style that fits the breed's demeanour.

A Coat of White

Like many breeds, the Bichon is a double-coated dog, and the standard describes how the dual-layered fur should look and feel. Stroking a Bichon should delight the hands, and the velvety

Heads Up

The Bichon's head is not carried forward when he moves, but is instead held up, which lends to the appearance of an attentive and lively dog.

The Bichon tail should curve gracefully over the back in a stylish plume of fur.

curls do just that. The white coat is surprisingly thick, similar to velvet, and the hair is full-bodied with coarse curl. Beneath the puff is the softer fluff that makes the coat stand away from the body.

In the show ring, a Bichon must be trimmed to show his naturally curvy shape, but without the cut following the exact shape of the body. The Bichon has no harsh angles and neither should his trim. The lines of the cut should be round on head and legs, and the back trim should be level, with the overall shape illustrating the breed's powderpuff appearance (see Chapter 5 for more information on grooming).

The colour of the Bichon is white, but cream or apricot markings are acceptable up to 18 months. The pigmentation beneath the coat is dark; black, blue or beige markings are often found on the skin.

Temperament

The temperament should always be considered one of the most important points. A Bichon without that cheerful countenance is almost not a Bichon. Personality is one of the key assets of the breed.

The outside appearance of the Bichon should be merely the reflection of his heart and soul. These born-to-be-companion dogs should be in harmony with and considerate of their people's moods. The Bichon should be the best of all moods: quiet, cuddly, upbeat, lively, extroverted, polite. Most of all, a well-bred, carefully

The Show Trim

In the show ring, a Bichon must be trimmed to show his naturally curvy shape, but without the cut following the exact shape of the body — the Bichon has no harsh angles and neither should his trim.

nurtured and loved Bichon should be a happy member of your family who brings joy and delight to those around him.

To read the complete Kennel Club and American Kennel Club standards for the Bichon Frise, see the Appendix.

IS A BICHON BEST FOR YOU?

Because they love people so much, Bichons usually adapt well to just about any home and eagerly love anybody who loves them. This trait is just one of many that make the Bichon a good pet. But are you the kind of person who can provide the best home for a Bichon?

What does it take to make a good Bichon owner? First, potential owners must live by the credo that getting a dog means a lifetime commitment to that animal. Future owners should be dog wise in general and Bichon knowledgeable in particular. With the Bichon, this means understanding that this breed requires a huge commitment in personal time, grooming, financial expense, consistency in training, and a watchful eye toward health care.

Bichon Issues

Some issues Bichon owners face are:

- Extensive grooming
- Housetraining difficulty
- Attention needs
- Health issues

According to breed rescue volunteers, many people are attracted to the Bichon because of their happy faces and cute "stuffed toy" appearance, but have no idea how much work this breed takes. The Bichon is a dog like any other and, as such, requires a major investment on the part of the owner. With the Bichon, the need is greater than average because it is such a high-maintenance dog.

Choosing a Bichon as the perfect dog should include not only an appreciation for their looks and character, but also an awareness of their difficult traits and the ability to acknowledge and deal with them.

Endless Grooming

The coat doesn't naturally look like a perfect white powder puff—it must be groomed to give it that special Bichon style. Are you willing and able to brush your dog daily and bathe him at least every two weeks? Can you afford to take him to the groomer at least once a month? Or do you have the time and ability to learn to do all the

The Bichon's coat is his signature—white, thick, and silky.

Daily brushing will become part of your life as a Bichon owner.

grooming yourself?

Without the commitment to grooming, the Bichon coat will mat into an uncomfortable mess in a very short time. Don't get a Bichon just for his appearance, particularly if you aren't able to keep his coat in proper condition.

Housetraining

Rescue volunteers note that probably the main reason Bichons are given up is because of the difficulty in housetraining them. Some dog experts feel that the Bichon may be one of the hardest breeds to reliably housetrain. Why? There's no good answer; they just are. If you cannot live with this, the Bichon is not the right breed for you.

It is possible to train the Bichon not to relieve himself inappropriately indoors, but it takes a longer time than with some other breeds—as long as 6 to 18 months—and owners must be extremely vigilant about their training. Additionally, breeders who have successfully housetrained their Bichons are adamant about the necessity of using a crate to do so. People who do not wish to crate-train a new dog may do better with a different breed.

Even with a Bichon who does become properly housetrained, accidents will still occur. On bad weather days, or if he doesn't feel well, a Bichon may on occasion choose to relieve himself indoors. If this bothers you, or if your flooring won't hold up to periodic puddles, don't get a Bichon.

Lonesome Blues

As a dog whose function it is to be a companion, the Bichon has an intense need for interaction with his owner. In fact, his cheery disposition depends on being loved and being the centre of someone's world.

Bichons who are parted from their owners, particularly for longer periods of time, tend to develop behavioural problems. This can include destructive chewing, inappropriate soiling, barking and howling, and full-blown separation anxiety. They may also become shy or fearful, and housetraining becomes nearly impossible if you are away all day.

Owners who work outside the home for long hours, who travel frequently, or who are involved in extensive after-hours activities where they cannot take a dog, are not good candidates for a Bichon. People who cannot tolerate a dog who has to be *with* them— touching them—all the time, also should not consider this breed.

When it's time to go to bed at night, a Bichon's preferred sleeping spot will be in your bed, snuggled on the pillow beside you. He simply must be near his people. Ideally, the Bichon does best in a home where at least one person is home all the time, or where one family member comes home throughout the day.

Not only must they be close, they demand nearly constant demonstrations of affection. A Bichon will incessantly lick your face, lay on your feet, push your work aside to get petted, and climb in your lap while you're typing on the computer. They are a dependent, in-your-face breed, and an owner who is not the touchy-feely type will not appreciate a Bichon. If you're expecting a dog who will lie contentedly at your feet and stay off the furniture, consider another breed.

Close to You

Bichons are often fondly referred to by their owners as "ankle Velcro," or their "shadow."

Timetables

Most Bichons prefer to live a life that is well-ordered, thriving on schedules for meal and exercise times. If your Bichon should be one of those who has bladder problems, an upset in his schedule can result not only in housetraining issues, but can cause health conditions to flare, which may require medical treatment.

Even if you are able to provide a Bichon with the attention he needs, if your schedule changes frequently or is inconsistent from week to week, this may stress a routine-loving Bichon into anxious behaviour that is unacceptable to you.

Health

Despite the fact that the Bichon is a sturdy little dog who is normally healthy, the breed is prone to certain chronic health conditions (see Chapter 8 for more information). These conditions—allergies, urinary conditions, orthopedic problems—can be expensive to treat. Moreover, they may call for changes in lifestyle that can

Bichons demand nearly constant demonstrations of affection.

Because of their small size, Bichons are happy in a small house or a flat.

affect members of your household, not just the dog.

Chronic health problems also can mean sleepless nights for owners, cancellation of plans, changing schedules to go to the vet's, and the expenditure of funds that may have been intended for a special holiday or even for paying bills. Individuals who can't afford to provide the ongoing medical care some Bichons need, and who don't have flexible personal or work schedules to provide this care, might do better without a Bichon.

The good news is that the Bichon is a long-lived breed. Many owners report that their dogs have lived to be 14, 15, and some as old as 17 years. With this type of longevity, the Bichon does not start to show signs of aging until between 10 and 12 years of age. For those who want a long-lived companion, the Bichon is an excellent choice.

Living Arrangements

Because of their small size, Bichons make good city dogs. In the urban jungle, they fare well since they can be paper- or litterbox-trained. But they are equally as happy in suburbia or down on the farm. In the farmyard though, because of their small size, care should be taken to keep a Bichon out from under the feet of large animals.

Indoors, any space will satisfy their needs as long as you are there. One consideration is that the environment should be low in dust, mould, or other allergens due to the breed's predisposition toward allergies. It's difficult to control outdoor allergens, but if you live in an area where mould or pollen is exceptionally high, as in a heavily wooded area, or where air and water are regularly exposed to chemical pollutants, an allergy-prone Bichon might experience more problems in this type of environment.

One advantage to the Bichon's difficult coat is its low incidence of shedding or moulting. All dogs do shed to some degree, but the Bichon is an infrequent shedder who drops very little coat. Although clothes and furniture will not be entirely free of dog fur, if you prefer not to be covered with your dog's hair, the Bichon may be an excellent choice.

Coat Fact

TThe Bichon's coat is high maintenance, but the plus point is that it sheds very little.

Outside the House

Just about any dog does better with a fenced garden, but it is not a necessity with the Bichon. They are home-loving dogs and have no great desire to go exploring. Although a romp in the dirt is fun to any dog, Bichons aren't big diggers and can be allowed near prized flower beds, as long as they are supervised around poisonous plants.

Extremes in temperatures, particularly very hot or humid climates are not a deterrent to getting a Bichon, but the dog does do better in moderate or cooler climes. Humidity can cause coat matting and exacerbation of allergies, as can high, dry temperatures. Outings in the snow can result in snowballs collecting in the curly coat, which can also result in mats.

Hypoallergenic Coat

Despite their own tendency towards allergies, Bichons themselves have a low likelihood of provoking an allergic response in people. For a person with allergies who wants a dog, the Bichon may be the breed to consider.

However, the Bichon should not be deemed to *never* cause allergic reactions. Individuals with allergies should spend time around these dogs first to see if the fur, dandruff, or saliva causes any reaction. If not, it might be all right to get a Bichon, with your doctor's approval.

Another caution: If your condition is likely to change, don't get a dog who you may later be forced to give up if your allergies worsen. This isn't fair to you or your dog.

Family...

One of the most important considerations when picking a dog is the family with whom he will be living. Do all family members want a dog? Can every individual help with the dog's care, or can they abide by the rules that govern dog care and training? If everyone is not thrilled with the idea of getting a dog, or is not interested in helping with the care, then you may be better off not adding a furry family member.

Is your household noisy, with loud sounds that may startle a dog and cause nervous or fearful behaviour? Is everyone healthy enough to interact with a dog? Are you about to undergo a major life change such as a move, career change, divorce, or birth of a baby? If your family or home environment is shifting in major directions at the present, wait for a calmer time to get a dog.

Children

Are there children in your home, and are they old enough to respect a dog as a living creature and not a toy? Although Bichons get along quite well with children as playmates, many breeders will not place a puppy in a home that has children under the age of 8 years. The younger the child, the more likely it is that he may accidentally injure a dog, particularly a small dog like the Bichon.

After housetraining, volunteers estimate that another big reason Bichons are turned over to rescue is for growling and snapping at children. In most cases, these dogs have come out of homes where they've experienced a history of rough handling and injury by young children. The natural canine response is to engage in defensive warning behaviour or biting. Caution is advised when bringing a Bichon into a home with youngsters: Whenever children and dogs are together, they must be supervised. Children should learn how to play with the dog in a gentle manner, and parents should see that the dog is behaving acceptably toward the children.

Elderly People

Bichons make great companions for older people. The Bichon's love of cuddling, and the ability to exercise him without extensive physical effort makes him an ideal housemate. However, there are a couple of points to consider. For those on a limited, fixed income, the expenses involved in grooming a Bichon may prove prohibitive. Also, with the breed's housetraining issues, for a person who is physically unable to keep up with a need for frequent trips outdoors, the Bichon may not be the best choice.

People With Special Needs

When you hear the term "special needs," it usually refers to someone who needs extra care because of a physical condition, chronic disease, or emotional issue. As a dog who is aware of and sensitive to the concerns of his people, the Bichon may make an ideal dog for the person with special needs.

Some Bichon owners have autistic children, family members with cancer or Alzheimer's disease, or themselves have disabling physical problems like hearing difficulties, heart disease, depression, and more. These owners recount stories about how their Bichons assist them physically and provide emotional support. It is as if the Bichon has a special ability to relate to the more vulnerable people in our society.

The Bichon also makes an excellent PAT (Pets As Therapy) dog, visiting hospital patients and residents in long-stay establishments. For more information, see page 150.

Introducing Kids and Dogs

- Demonstrate with a stuffed toy how to safely and carefully handle a puppy. Have your children practice holding and petting the toy animal.

- When your new dog and children meet for the first time, an adult should calmly hold the puppy while the kids quietly and slowly approach. Allow the pup to smell the back of their partially closed hand first. Then they may gently pet him.

- Children must not be allowed to handle a Bichon roughly. Don't let them pinch or poke him, or pull his tail, ears, or legs. Teach them not to step on or drop the dog, or squeeze him tightly. Never let your child hit the dog.

- Instruct your children not to stare, bark, or growl at the dog, even if they are only playing. They should leave him alone while he is eating or sleeping, and avoid startling him. This can cause your Bichon to feel threatened and he may react by growling, snapping, or biting.

- Never make a child responsible for a dog's care, although they can and should help when they are old enough.

- Show your children how to nurture and respect your Bichon; show them by example.

... and Friends

Friendliness is a nice trait in the Bichon. Your family's friends will be your dog's friends, too. Bichons greet guests as enthusiastically as they greet you, as long as they are properly socialised. Dogs who are isolated may bark at visitors to warn of an intrusion into their territory, or they may hide in fear and be miserable every time company comes. Those without training may jump all over your guests and make them want to leave before their visit even begins.

Bichons make great companions for older people.

Regardless of training and friendliness, some people do not like or do not want to be around dogs. Once you add a dog to your family, these people may not come to see you anymore. Additionally, although you may take your Bichon with you wherever you go, not everyone will appreciate a doggy visitor—ask before taking your dog on visits. With a network of Bichon lovers easily contacted through the Internet, you can make new friends where both you and your dog can enjoy the company of others with mutual interests.

Other Pets

The Bichon is generally considered to be a non-aggressive breed with a low prey drive (the instinctive desire to chase and kill small game). As such, this dog usually gets along well with other pets. This includes more than cats and other dogs. Owners tell how their Bichons watch over gerbils, rabbits, and even birds.

Because of their need for companionship, Bichons usually do better in a home shared with other animals. However, the small Bichon could be easily hurt by a large dog. If you have a large dog and want to add a Bichon, the larger dog should be friendly and gentle-mannered. Before adopting a Bichon, it might be advisable for the two dogs to meet to make certain they will get along. And, when they are first learning to live together, their play should always be supervised until you are certain the larger dog will not accidentally injure your Bichon.

Bichons also can live well with cats, but preferably one that is dog friendly. Just as you would carefully introduce and supervise the play when meeting a new dog, the same holds true for cats. Go slowly, and watch them together before allowing them to play alone. A scratch from a large cat could hurt a little Bichon.

Not only do Bichons prefer to be around their people all the time, they also like the company of other animals. When breeders and rescue coordinators place Bichons in a home, they prefer to do so where another Bichon already lives. These dogs seem to do better in pairs in most situations. If you already have other friendly pets, the Bichon could make a nice addition to your home.

Weekend Warriors

Are you the kind of person who spends every weekend mountain biking and weeknights jogging several miles, with dreams of a dog by your side during your adventures? If so, the Bichon is probably not the best dog for your active lifestyle. Because of their small size and possible orthopedic problems, high-impact or endurance sports are not best for this breed. But if you like leisurely walks on the beach or the occasional stroll in the park, then a Bichon may be the perfect exercise companion.

Of course, every dog needs frequent exercise as part of his regular care, but some breeds require more than others. The Bichon is a high-energy dog, but his exercise needs can be easily met by a

Supervise play until you are certain your larger dog will not accidentally injure your Bichon.

daily walk, a romp in the garden, or a game of catch in the house on rainy days.

Introducing New Pets

When pet-to-pet introductions are not done properly, the fur can fly when first they meet. Here are some steps to help your new and old pets start off on the right paw together:

- Don't bring home a Bichon if you already have a pet who cannot accept or get along with a new dog.

- If you have multiple pets at home, introduce your new Bichon to them one at a time, beginning with the alpha (head) dog or cat. Put your new dog in his crate and your existing dog on lead. Allow them to see and smell each other.

- After a few days, when the excitement dies down and the existing pet sees that the new one is here to stay, you can let them get closer, but have one person restrain each animal while they are getting used to each other. Always supervise all contact until you are certain they can get along without fighting.

- Never do introductions at mealtime. Separate the animals when they are eating.

- Each pet must have his own food, bowls, bed, and crate. Your existing pet must understand that he will still get enough to eat and prized toys will not be given to the newcomer. Let the older pets know they are still loved without showing favouritism to one animal over another.

- The adjustment of older pets to a new Bichon will not happen overnight. Introductions should be done slowly, over a period of at least 1 to 2 weeks. Acceptance may take longer.

During puppyhood, the Bichon can be wildly active, barely slowing down long enough to eat and sleep. As he matures, this whirlwind of energy will slow down to intermittent bursts of playfulness, with quiet times in between when his preferred activity is snuggling with his human.

Don't rule out the Bichon just because you have a very active or sedentary lifestyle. A little increase in exercise could be good for you. Or maybe you can channel some of your playtime into a competitive dog sport, like agility, which you can do with your dog.

PERSONALITY PLUS

Ask people what it is they love about the Bichon and they can talk for hours about the endearing behaviour of their dogs. Even the technical language of the breed's standard waxes poetic when describing the Bichon personality using the words gay, happy, lively, friendly and outgoing.

Clowning Around

The Bichon's outlook on life is like looking up the word "happy" in a thesaurus—merry, gay, jaunty, perky, mirthful, exuberant, bright—words that only begin to capture the essence of this fun-loving, playful breed. Some might see this dog as a daily dose of Prozac in a fuzzy white package.

These little clowns have a sense of humour and mischief, and enjoy playing tricks on their people and other animals. They like to trick their owners into looking away while they steal small objects and hide them. They team up to get what they want, they love to rummage around in the rubbish, and they like taking each other's toys.

A competitive dog sport, like agility, might be a fun way to exercise your Bichon.

But the Bichon's capacity to cheer does not stop with their antics. Owners repeatedly describe them as sensitive, intuitive, and compassionate. Bichons sense when something is wrong, respond with loving concern, and seek to provide comfort by smiling, kissing, or just cuddling. The breed has a reputation for staying by their people's sides when they are ill, or for licking away tears when they cry.

Love Me!

Many a love song could have been written about the Bichon's deep need to love and be loved, with their version sounding something like, "Ooo I need your love, hope you need my love too, love me, hold me, never let me go."

Most dogs take their "jobs" seriously. Border Collies love to herd, but Bichons live to love. Born and bred to be a companion, without this fundamental purpose in their lives, these dogs are lost. The breed is notoriously affectionate, clinging to their humans with a steadfastness that is unshakable.

A Bichon will let almost nothing stop his drive to perform his function of loving his people. While you're working on the computer, he'll be in your lap; stand at the kitchen sink, he'll lie on your feet; sit down to read the paper or lay down for a nap, and he'll snuggle against your side. If you leave him alone, he'll howl out a mournful tune until his "lost" love returns, then greet you at the door with unrepressed enthusiasm.

Bichons become excited when they see another Bichon, and are eager to make friends.

Should Old Acquaintance Be Forgot

A friendly Bichon loves to make new friends, and old ones are never forgotten. Once the Bichon has the pleasure of making someone's acquaintance, he will recognise that person, even though years may have passed since he last saw them.

Bichons also recognise their own kind. While they may be happy to meet and play with other dogs, they seem to prefer small white dogs as playmates. But they really get ecstatic when they see another Bichon. Owners tell how their dogs become excited when they see another Bichon, and are eager to make friends.

Drama Queens and Kings

Wherever they go, Bichons command attention with their endearing looks and captivating faces. Their attitude is that they are worthy of adoration and admiration from everyone around them. It is inconceivable to the Bichon that he is not loved by all.

They are born entertainers—some like to perform and will engage in clever antics to gain attention and applause. "They'll do anything to make you laugh," says Carol Watt, owner of a 4-year-old Bichon.

They also like to please—if the activity is something they want to do and food is involved. But a request to do something they do not want to do may be met with stubborn resistance or a response so cute you'll have to laugh instead of pursuing your request.

Beside being a bit theatrical, the Bichon is portrayed as being

Don't Go!

"Buttons and Beau get sad when they see me getting ready to leave. Beau follows me around and cries. Buttons hides, and peeks out with that 'cute look' to try to get me to stay," a Bichon lover relates. "When I come home, they will greet me, but then Beau gets upset that I was away and ignores me. After he's decided he's ignored me enough, he wakes me up in the middle of the night with kisses."

a highly emotional dog. While not prone to excessive dramatics, Bichons express a wide variety of emotions to their owners—love, of course, but also anger, jealousy, pride, embarrassment, and sadness. Owners also note that they can be a bit vindictive if they are unhappy with you.

Bichons know how to manipulate their owners to get what they want. A cute look may be all it takes. Or they may push their owners with their heads, or take them by the hand to lead them towards the toy or food for which they are asking. Because of their intensely emotional nature, many owners feel their Bichons are "human-like" or "almost human." The dog's capacity for deep love is another reason they think this way. Many owners see their Bichon as part of their soul.

However the drama of daily life unfolds, the Bichon wants to participate. As long as he is beside you, involved in your activities, and sharing your love, he will be one happy dog.

Behaviour Bits

Since they are so loaded with looks and personality, what more does the Bichon need? Probably nothing, but they do have a few traits that add even more charm to their character.

Blitzing

Also called "puppy madness," or "buzzing," the Bichon blitz is when one or more Bichons get up and tear around the house or yard as fast as they can, often barking nonstop as they run.

- Blitzing stops as suddenly as it begins, with a very satisfied and smiling dog collapsing on the floor with a sigh. Why blitz?
- Triggers may be an extremely happy mood or an intense desire for wild play.

The Wave

The "wave" is a Bichon special move in which the dog stands up on his hind legs and pumps both front legs up and down simultaneously in a waving motion. This move was made famous by the American Westminster winner JR, when he sat in his trophy and did the wave in front of millions of TV viewers.

The wave is a special Bichon move, where the dog stands up on his hind legs and pumps both front legs up and down simultaneously in a waving motion.

Bichons love to steal kisses.

What makes the wave special is that it is not a learned behaviour, but one that a portion of all Bichons do without any prompting or instruction. The spontaneous trick is used when they beg for a treat, ask for attention, or express extreme excitement.

Some breed historians believe the wave may trace its roots to the days when Bichons helped earn their owner's keep as dancing dogs. Some owners believe that Bichons, as emotional dogs, have a joy in life that they express through the wave.

Kissing Bandits

Many owners describe the Bichon's penchant for stealing. The trick is to get you to look in the other direction while they make off with socks, pens, and anything small that is within reach.

They also love to steal kisses, but not just one. Bichons are dedicated lickers. Next to cuddling, licking the faces of the people they love and like may be a favourite pastime of these affectionate dogs. For owners who don't appreciate having their face thoroughly washed every time their Bichon is in the mood, the licks can be redirected to hands, wrists, or even favourite toys.

Super Smile

Every dog lover will tell you plainly that, yes, dogs do indeed smile. To the Bichon owner, this breed's smile outshines all others. The Bichon grin is so radiant partly because of the way the bright white face emphasises their black lips, nose, and eyes. But, this dog simply loves to smile and, when he does, it's a smile from the heart that lights up his eyes and expresses his delight.

A Dog by Any Other Name

Most people have nicknames for their dogs, but the Bichon is so special the whole breed has nicknames. Bichons may affectionately be referred to as Fluffs, Flufferbutts, or Fluffers.

IT'S NOT ALL FUN AND GAMES: THE DOWNSIDE OF DOGS

Life with a dog is an enriching and rewarding experience, but it's not without its difficulties. If a Bichon is going to be your first venture into the company of canines, be prepared to accept new limitations and extra duties. It is important to weigh up the pros and cons before making a final decision.

- **Time and commitment**. Dogs need at least 1 to 2 hours every day for their care. Your dog's schedule may not always be convenient for you. Having a dog means accommodating his needs. When you are tired, busy, or sick, your dog still requires care.

- **Budgetary concerns**. Dogs always cost more than you think they will, and unforeseen expenses can come at the worst times. If you must decide between spending money on yourself or your dog, the dog's needs must come before personal wants.

- **Continuing education**. Education about canine health and behaviour never ends. Training your dog to maintain manners is a daily undertaking.

- **Constant vigilance**. Your dog always needs your supervision to keep him safe and out of trouble. You should know where he is and what he is doing at all times.

- **Life with a dog is messy**. You will have to clean up vomit and urine, and scoop poop. Even as minimal shedders, Bichons will leave fur on your clothing and furniture. They will leave muddy paw prints and nose prints on doors. And dogs don't put away their toys.

- **Dog ownership can be tedious and trying at times.** However, it's not okay to exchange your dog for an easier "hobby."Owners should realise that caring for puppies, coping with behavioural problems, or looking after ill, injured, or elderly dogs is difficult. Just because the relationship gets rough doesn't mean you can abandon your dog. A commitment to a Bichon must be honoured for his lifetime.

3

PREPARING
for Your Bichon Frise

S o, you've made the decision to get a dog. After careful, thorough consideration, you have determined that you have the time, energy, patience, and financial resources essential for a lifelong commitment to a canine companion.

Even better, you know it's the Bichon Frise you want—nearly everything about their looks and personality appeals to you more than any other breed. You've decided that the extra effort of grooming and housetraining a Bichon are worth it. And you're willing to learn all the information you need to provide him with the best home possible.

WHAT KIND OF BICHON IS BEST?

You'll have to make just a few more decisions before you go out and find the Bichon of your dreams.

Mister or Miss?

Do you want a male or female Bichon? Each sex is lovable and loving in return, but subtle differences do exist. Females may be moodier. Males may be rowdier. Both are affectionate, but while males are unashamedly sweet about cuddle time, females can be more independent and demanding of affection on their own terms. In contrast to many breeds, Bichon females may be more dominant and manipulative about getting their way. They also tend to bark a little more, but may learn more quickly—except in housetraining, where some owners believe that males become more reliable about housetraining. In general, differences are minor, and both males and females make wonderful companions.

Puppy or Adult?

One of the biggest decisions you'll have to make is whether to get a puppy or an adult dog. Both will require your love, time, and attention, but the similarities stop there. Puppies tug at your heartstrings with their extra-cute looks and mannerisms. Those same

One of the biggest decisions you'll have to make is whether to get a puppy or an adult dog.

mannerisms are what make them a handful to rear. They cry, bark, chew, get into trouble, don't sleep, and need to eat and relieve themselves almost all the time. They have to be trained, supervised, and are a never-ending job the first few months of their lives. The maxim about puppies is that most owners can't wait for them to grow up, but then they fondly recall and miss their dog's puppyhood after he is grown.

Even though adult dogs also require care, they don't demand the constant attention that a puppy does. They tend to be calmer and have more training already in place. With a mature dog, you know exactly what you're getting—not always a given with even the best bred and chosen puppy. With a puppy, you can train him into what you hope he will be as he grows; an adult may just need some brushing up on manners, but he may have already developed his own personality. Consider the options and decide what is best for your family, and to which age of Bichon you can provide the best home. Whichever your preference, an adult dog will bond to his new family just as closely as a puppy would.

Dogs Are Individuals

Male or female, adult or puppy, show or pet, remember when choosing your Bichon that each dog is an individual. Genetics, environment, and training all affect the development of his personality, but each makes for a special, unique companion to love.

Show Dog or Family Companion?

Is your Bichon going to be the star of your home, or do you have hopeful plans of having a star in the show ring? Either will still be a loving companion, but the show Bichon will need extra care, expenditures, training, and time to embark on a career. Considerations in choosing a show-quality dog require more research and planning. If you think you might want to try your hand in conformation competition, look for breeders who have bred multiple Champions. Talk to them at length, and enlist their aid in choosing the right show puppy for you.

WHERE TO FIND THE BICHON FRISE OF YOUR DREAMS

Once you've determined what type of Bichon is the best match for your lifestyle, the most important criteria is still to be met: Where will you get your dog? So many puppies and dogs are being offered for sale or placement these days that the choice is overwhelming. From ads on the Internet, in magazines, and local newspapers to breeders, rehoming centres, rescue groups or owner give-ups—how do you choose a safe, reliable method for obtaining your family's pet?

Breeders

The first place to look for a breeder and see quality Bichons in action at the same time is at a dog show. Breeders and owners there can answer your questions (*after* they have finished showing) about the breed, their breeding programme, any puppies they have, or about upcoming litters. Catalogues can be purchased at the show that list the names and addresses of owner-breeders so that you can also contact them after a show.

Breeders may also be found online or through national dog

Bichon Plus

Not all dogs in breed rescue will be 100 percent purebred but, in most groups, they will be a least half Bichon.

Visiting the breeder gives you a chance to see the dam and watch the puppies in their home environment.

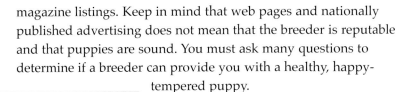

magazine listings. Keep in mind that web pages and nationally published advertising does not mean that the breeder is reputable and that puppies are sound. You must ask many questions to determine if a breeder can provide you with a healthy, happy-tempered puppy.

Beware of Bad Breeders

Despite an irresistible fluffy face that promises love, buying a puppy from a breeder with a less than sterling reputation is a promise of heartbreak in days to come. Signs that you should keep looking for a puppy from a different breeder might include:

- Breeder has several types of dogs, lots of puppies, or has many litters every year.
- Advertises only in small or local newspapers or neighbourhood newsletters, or only on the Internet on sites that list too many dogs for sale to anyone who has the money.
- Puppies who are under 8 weeks of age and described as "ready to go."
- Prices that are too low to be believable. And, unless you're buying a very special show-quality dog, prices that are too high are not an indication of an exceptional dog, just of exceptional greed.
- The breeder is not insistent on having puppies returned, or the breeder explicitly tells you she will not take the puppy back should you be unable to keep him.
- When you visit, the mother or the puppies are shy, fearful, or nasty tempered, in poor condition, or appear sick or listless. Also, be wary if the mother cannot be viewed or if information about the sire is withheld.
- Kennel Club papers are unavailable because the litter does not qualify for registration for some reason.
- Breeder won't provide you with references.
- Breeder withholds health or history data, or blatantly denies the existence of obviously noticeable health problems.
- Breeder does not actually have the dam, sire, or the puppies; only buys puppies from other "breeders" and resells them, usually via the Internet; offered as a puppy locator service.

Questions To Ask the Breeder

When interviewing a breeder, keep in mind that a good breeder who does her job correctly does not breed for income but for the betterment of the breed. As a matter of fact, reputable breeders tend to lose money on their litters because their work is about the puppies, not about profit.

Questions to ask a potential breeder centre on the dogs' health history and her purchase policies. How far back in a litter's pedigree have health histories been checked and cleared? For what genetic defects does she test and strive to eliminate in her breeding programme? Due to the increased occurrence of certain inherited diseases and conditions in the Bichon, parents, grandparents, and preferably great-grandparents should have been examined for the incidence of conditions such as cataracts and luxating patellas which occur in Bichons (see chapter 8).

You will want to make an appointment to visit the breeder so that you can see the puppies in their home environment. It will also give you a chance to see the dam and get information about the sire. If a breeder doesn't want you to visit, this could be a signal that she has something to hide. When you visit, take a look around: Are the dogs and their area clean and well-kept?

Find out the condition of the mother and the puppies: Are they all healthy? What type of a health guarantee does the breeder provide? Is she willing to take the puppy back or assist you if problems arise? Are puppy prices reasonable for the quality of the litter? Are they too low or too high, or comparable to prices charged by other reputable breeders? Ask for references from her previous puppy buyers.

Questions a Breeder Will Ask You

Expect to provide personal references to the breeder. Be prepared to be interrogated. If the breeder doesn't ask questions of you, this too should be a warning sign. Don't be offended when the breeder thoroughly quizzes you on your dog knowledge and experience, as well as asks you about your family, lifestyle, finances, and living facilities. A caring breeder should ask about your ability to provide for one of her puppies, your plans for the puppy, if your home and family are suitable both physically and emotionally for a puppy, and if you are willing to make a lifetime commitment to the welfare of a new dog.

Paperwork

When both parties satisfy the other's requirements, and a special puppy has picked you out, you will need to sort out the paperwork. Some breeders will ask you to sign a contract, which will stipulate your obligations toward the puppy and the return of the dog if you no longer can provide a good home, along with a spay/neuter agreement, and the terms of the purchase. You should also receive from the breeder a complete veterinary and vaccine record), a copy of your puppy's pedigree, and a form for registering your puppy (more information on registration follows in this chapter).

Breeders who care about their dogs and work, care about your puppy for his lifetime. Contact your breeder if you have any questions about or problems with your Bichon. Chances are, your breeder will try to help.

Adoption Options

If you've decided you would like to adopt an adult Bichon, several options exist. Check with breeders to see if they have a retired show dog they would like to place. These dogs are most often outgoing, healthy dogs just looking for a retirement home away from the ring. Ask the same questions you would if you were looking for a puppy.

That Healthy Look

A healthy puppy looks like, well, like he's healthy. He should have:

- A shiny coat
- Bright, clear eyes
- A happy expression
- Pink gums and tongue
- An active energy level
- Firm stools of a normal colour
- That indefinable puppy glow and sweet puppy breath

Without:

- Runny eyes or nose
- Stooped posture
- Lethargic appearance
- Dull coat
- Other signs that make you immediately think, "Ooh, that puppy looks sick."

Rescue

An option for finding a Bichon in serious need of a home is breed rescue. Rescue groups are coordinated by individual Bichon enthusiasts who have strong stomachs, soft hearts, generous purse strings, room in their households, unending patience, and tons of experience in caring for and retraining needy dogs. These dogs are surrendered or abandoned by owners, or picked up by concerned animal lovers and put into foster homes. In foster care, they receive veterinary testing and treatment, have their temperament evaluated for future placement, and are socialised and loved by the people with whom they are temporarily living.

Sadly, Bichon rescue always has more dogs than available homes. Former owners who are unable or unwilling to keep up with the grooming, or who can't deal with Bichon housetraining issues, or who are just incapable of providing the dog with the time and attention this breed requires in great quantities, are the primary reasons for abandonment. Other reasons include owners incapable of dealing with Bichon health problems or with dog behaviour in general. Death, divorce, loss of a job, or a move are more reasons.

Rescuing an adult Bichon can be a great option.

Whatever the reason, many wonderful Bichons are in rescue—one that may be just right for you.

Rescue dogs are usually 7 months of age and older. Some come with health conditions that need treated, others with training or minor behaviour issues that need work. Dogs with serious problems like aggression or biting are not offered for adoption through ethical rescue groups.

Adopting from a rescue group will not be the right option for every owner. But for those who are able to offer a special dog a little extra, rescue dogs pay off the effort in gratitude and love because they tend to bond very deeply to their new families.

To find a rescue group, search on the Internet for those closest to your area. Ask the same questions you would if you were buying a puppy from a breeder—and more. While much background can never be known about a rescued Bichon, get as detailed a recent history as possible from the dog's foster home. Be guided by the rescue volunteers in selecting a dog who is best suited for your home and lifestyle.

Rescue dogs do not come free. Just because they were someone else's throw-aways does not mean they are without value. Adoption fees are usually higher than in all-breed rehoming centres, but less than purchasing a puppy. These fees cover foster, placement, and medical expenses such as neutering and vaccinations.

To adopt a rescue Bichon, you will be required to fill out an application that determines if you can provide a suitable, loving home. The questions will ask about your experience with dogs and the breed, why you want a dog, your financial ability to provide care, your family size and activities, garden and household facilities, and much more. In some cases, a volunteer will come to your home for a pre-qualification interview. Standards set by the groups for potential owners are very high. Don't be upset—the goal of the rescue group is to make as near perfect a match as possible so that a Bichon once rescued should never be in need of rescue again.

Registering Your Bichon

The Kennel Club

When you purchase a Bichon puppy in the United Kingdom, registry for your dog will be through the Kennel Club. At the time a litter is born, the breeder registers the pups in the litter. Then, when you purchase one of those puppies, you will be given a certificate of registration and ownership. The breeder will provide you with a portion of this form, which must be filled out and submitted. Completion and acceptance will transfer ownership of the registered puppy. Ownership must be transferred in order to participate in any Kennel Club-regulated dog sporting events. More information can be found at www.the-kennel-club.org.uk/

Animal Shelters

In all rehoming centres there is a surprising number of pedigree dogs. Bichons are relatively rare, as most seem to be given to specialist rescue groups. However, Bichons are found in the bigger rehoming centres occasionally.

The staff will provide you with information about dogs that need rehoming, but this may be limited to where the dog was picked up or if the owners brought him in. Medical history will also probably be unknown. Before you adopt a Bichon from a rescue centre, make sure you are prepared and able to deal with medical or behavioural issues, because many of these are special-needs dogs.

While some people may view rescue dogs as nightmares waiting to happen, maybe you are one of those potential owners who

The efforts you put into researching your purchase or adoption will pay off with a healthier, more even-tempered dog in the end.

would like to give a Bichon the chance of finding a happy home, second time round. It is possible to find the Bichon of your dreams in a rehoming centre if you are willing to wait and work with the staff, and then to invest the time, money, knowledge, and effort needed to turn your new Bichon into a loving companion.

To find a rehoming centre in your area, check in the phone directory or use the Internet to check out the major UK dog charities.

Case History

Life-long dog-lover Jackie Morgan from Northumbria contacted her local Bichon rescue organisation when she and her husband were looking for a new dog. Her experience demonstrates how rewarding it can be to give a rescue dog a second chance.

Jackie says, "Both my husband and I are dog-lovers, but for several years we couldn't have a dog because we didn't have the right lifestyle. When we both found permanent jobs in Northumbria and bought our first house, we knew it was the ideal opportunity to bring a dog in to our lives once more. I always liked the idea of owning a Bichon, and we both wanted to give a dog a second chance, so we decided that we would contact our local

Bichon rescue organisation.

"After answering some questions about our lifestyles, and the sort of dog we were looking for, the rescue co-ordinator told us about two dogs she thought would suit us. One was a six-month-old male puppy, called Hector, who seemed ideal. The second was an older bitch called Lily, who, despite being older than we had in mind, was well suited in every other way. We agreed to see both, but privately thought that Hector was the dog for us—we really wanted a puppy or younger dog, one that would adapt easily to it's new life with us.

"We saw Hector first and thought we'd found our dog, but we agreed to see the older Lily as well. Whereas Hector was bouncing enthusiasm, Lily was quiet affection. She'd belonged to an old lady who had given her to a rescue centre when she made the decision to move to a residential home. Lily had never had any behavioural problems, was fully house-trained, walked well on a lead, and answered basic commands such as "Sit" and Come". Her only 'fault' was a tendency to be a little over-timid.

"My husband and I felt torn. Hector was perfect for us but my heart-strings had been well and truly tugged by little Lily. We asked the co-ordinator if we could think about it. The next day, we had made our decision. Not entirely convinced it was the right move, we had agreed to take on Lily, and that day we took her home.

For the first few days, Lily needed quite a lot of reassurance. She followed us everywhere in the house. By the end of the first week though, her personality was starting to flourish, and from then on she never looked back. We established a regular routine from the first day, and Lily adapted to it almost instantly. She never had an accident in the house, she was a joy to take for walks, and she preferred to spend most of her time snuggled on the sofa with us. Very soon, we couldn't imagine life without her.

A rescue dog will bond deeply with his new family.

What Registration Does (and Doesn't) Mean

When you buy a Bichon, his heritage is what is represented in registration with a recognised organisation like the KC or AKC. Other similar, reputable organisations exist. In the United States, this includes the United Kennel Club (UKC) and, in Europe, the Fédération Cynologique Internationale (FCI).

But registration isn't a guarantee of any type. Registration is not a guarantee of a breeder's ethics or practices. It is no indication of the health, temperament, or quality of any litter or puppy.

And registration is not a status symbol! Beware of a breeder who touts recognised registration as one of the most valuable reasons to buy her puppies. Registration with a recognised kennel club is important, but it should not be the most important factor when you decide which dog to buy.

Caveat Emptor

Buying a Bichon will go more smoothly if you analyse your options about from whom and where you buy a dog. Over his lifetime, efforts put into researching your purchase or adoption first will pay off with a healthier, more even-tempered dog in the end. Because dogs are family members, when there's a problem with them, it's not the same as when something goes wrong with a dishwasher or car. When your dog hurts, you hurt; you can't just "repair" or replace a dog and move on without consequence.

As the old saying goes—even when it comes to dogs—*caveat emptor*, or "buyer beware." Be thoroughly convinced that you are getting the right dog from the right provider before you make the commitment to buy or adopt. Don't neglect to ask questions because you don't want to offend someone who has a Bichon available. Don't skip getting the paperwork you need or overlook provisions in a contract that aren't what's best for you and your future dog.

"It's been four years since we took on Lily, and it's one of the best decisions we've ever made. We'd definitely recommend other would-be dog owners to consider this option rather than going straight for a puppy from a breeder. Many rescue dogs are just too good to miss!"

BRINGING HOME BICHON

You've found the perfect puppy. You'll be bringing him home in a few days, so you need to get ready for the big event.

Puppy Prep Your Home

Because of their bright, inquisitive personalities, Bichon puppies can be adept at getting into trouble, chewing dangerous objects, or shredding personal belongings that should be off limits to tiny teeth. In a matter of minutes, a single, small pup can cause hundreds of pounds worth of damage, and seriously injure himself in the process.

If you don't want your Bichon's first days home to be a series of reprimands, "No. Leave that alone. Get out of there. Drop that. Stop it. No!" then puppy-proof your house and garden before he arrives. Think of it as child-proofing your home, except that your puppy is smaller and more active than a baby and has easier, quicker access to items at his level.

Position baby gates across doorways into areas where your puppy isn't allowed. Close cabinets, drawers, and doors to rooms or storage spaces where he could get into trouble. Since a puppy believes that it's okay to chew anything that is within reach, provide plenty of toys for his busy little mouth. Always keep a close eye on what he is doing, no matter how well you have prepared your home for his arrival.

Pick up, put out of reach, secure, or keep your Bichon away from:
- Electrical and telephone wires, and computer cables
- Drawstrings from curtains or blinds, throw pillows, arm covers from chairs, and throw rugs
- Television and other remote controls, DVDs, CDs, video or cassette tapes
- Knick-knacks, figurines, or collectibles, candles, potpourri, and air fresheners, including the plug-in types
- Houseplants, some of which are poisonous, including the dead leaves

A baby gate can keep your Bichon safe and out of trouble.

- Medications, drugs, toiletries, cosmetics, combs, toothbrushes, hair ribbons or scrunchies, hair pins, and jewellery
- Heavy items like lamps that can get pulled down or knocked over on to your tiny Bichon
- Food, crumbs, bones or discarded cooking items. Also keep your puppy's own food and treats out of reach, as he could easily over-indulge
- Rubbish bins and litter bins, debris from fireplaces, firewood, and kindling
- Pens, pencils, crayons, markers, paper clips, rubber bands, tacks, staples, tape, and paper shredding machines, books, magazines, mail, newspapers, important documents, and money (paper or coin)
- Paper towels and napkins, tissues, toilet paper, roll cores, cleaning items, rags, sponges, household chemicals, and detergents
- Dirty laundry, shoes, socks, hats, scarves, and gloves
- Tools, nails, string, fasteners, glue, craft and sewing items, and scissors
- Children's toys, sporting equipment, and fishing gear
- Large items that cannot be moved out of reach, like chair or table legs, cabinet doors, doorstops or corner trim can be treated with a product that discourages chewing.

Once you've puppy-proofed the inside of your home, prepare the garden so that it is safe for your Bichon.

Safety Tip

Because attics and garages may contain so many hazardous objects, it's usually best to keep your puppy out of these areas at all times.

Make sure your yard is safe for your Bichon.

- Check fencing for weak or broken areas where your puppy could escape. Make necessary repairs and secure the bottom of the fence to the ground. Put padlocks on the fence gates.
- Remove poisonous shrubs and flowers. Use the Internet to find a full list of plants that are poisonous to dogs.
- Avoid the use of fertilisers, pesticides, or herbicides on the ground. These chemicals can be absorbed through the skin of the feet or licked off the fur, which can result in serious poisoning or death. If you must treat an area with any of these chemicals, keep your pup off the lawn for at least 48 hours afterwards or until after a steady, rinsing rain.
- Don't leave gardening tools or mowing equipment lying around.
- Keep your puppy away from your swimming pool or pond.
- Scoop the poop from your puppy's toileting area!

When you think your home is a puppy-proof zone, go through each area again. Did you miss anything? Are there objects in which your puppy could get caught or that he could pull down or rip up? Ask yourself, "If I were a Bichon, would this be an interesting place to explore? Would this be fun to chew, shred, or hide?"

Once your house and garden are safe for your puppy, set up his crate and bowls in the area designated for him. Then, when you introduce him to his new environment, watch him happily settle into his new home.

Supplies

Do you like to shop? If so, then getting ready to bring home your new Bichon is a perfect reason for a shopping expedition. Get your home ready for your new companion by purchasing and preparing the following for him:

- **Books** with breed-specific information, a home-medical reference for dogs, puppy care, training, and canine behaviour books
- **Food, food and water bowls (two sets), food storage containers.** Bowls should be Bichon-sized and easy to clean. Stainless steel is the preferred choice of many breeders, but you may opt for the decorative ceramic style instead. Plastic bowls are not the best choice for Bichons, because owners report they discolour the dog's white coat. But if this is what you prefer, try to select a heavy, durable plastic that is chip and peel resistant, and dishwasher safe.
- **Crate, bedding, and bed.** You can use old blankets or towels as bedding, but you will find the synthetic fleece dog bedding more convenient. The crate should be large enough for your dog to stand up and turn around. It's alright to buy his adult-sized crate now, but block off the extra space with a crate divider until he's full grown. Plastic, wire, and soft-sided crates are all good selections. Plastic crates should be chew-resistant, and soft-sides should not have any zippers or objects inside that your puppy could chew off and swallow.
- **Toys, chew toys.** Look for toys that are safe for puppies, with no small pieces or parts that are easily removed and on which he could choke. Chewables should resist splintering.
- **Puppy collar and lead, identification tag** (more on the right types in Chapter 6).
- **Healthy, bite-sized treats for training and rewards.**
- **Baby gate; possibly an exercise pen.** Select a style that your dog won't easily knock down or over which he could climb or jump.
- **Sweater** if the weather is cold or snowy.
- **Cleaners**, disinfectants, odour neutraliser, air freshener, enzyme carpet cleaner; consider getting a hand-held spot cleaning machine.
- **Pooper-scooper tools**, large outdoor rubbish bags, old

A collar that fits is essential for your Bichon.

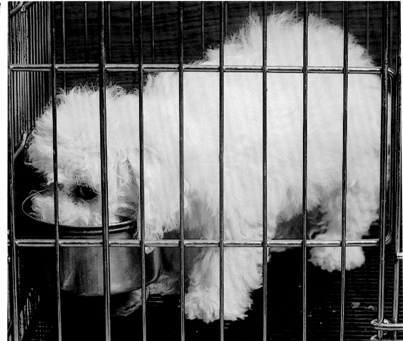

newspapers, and 'pick-up' bags (or nappy sacks).

- **Paper towels**, small indoor rubbish bags.
- **Puppy-resistant, indoor litter bins.**
- **Grooming tools and supplies** (more information in Chapter 5); towels for drying puppy if he gets wet outdoors.
- **Basket or container** for storing puppy's toys or supplies when he's not playing with them.
- **File** for keeping dog-related documents.

Identification

One of the most important items with which you should supply your pet is identification. Thousands of pets are lost each year, and only clear, current identification stands between them and a permanent path away from home. If you want your Bichon to get back to you should he become lost, make certain that he is well identified.

ID Tags

"Primary" identification is readily seen by anyone; it does not require special equipment or a need to search for the location of the identifier.

Engraved tags are the main way to provide primary ID for your dog. ID tags come in different shapes and sizes and are clipped on to collars. They can be purchased in pet supply stores and by mail order. It is essential that dogs wear ID tags at all times.

Permanent Identification

"Secondary" or permanent identification are those that cannot be removed or lost. This includes tattoos and microchips.

Dogs are usually tattooed on the inside of the ear, providing a permanent and visible form of ID. The number, along with the owner's address and telephone number and information about the dog, is registered with a national registry service or database, such as the National Dog Tattoo Register (www.dog-register.co.uk). No anaesthetic or sedation is required, and the procedure can be carried out on young puppies. In some cases, breeders will sell puppies that have already been tattooed.

Disadvantages to tattooing include the possibility that, as the dog grows and ages, the tattoo will stretch or fade until it is unrecognisable. Although most registration services have been combined into a central, single registry, a few separate registries still do not check with other sources.

Microchipping avoids most of the problems associated with tattooing. The procedure is more straightforward, and there is no risk of your dog suffering any discomfort. The microchip lasts for a lifetime, and the cost of registration is included in the price of the chip. In a few seconds, a vet can inject the rice-grain-sized, biologically inactive, sealed unit under the skin between a dog's shoulders. Chips, which do not contain chemicals or batteries, are then easily read via a hand-held scanner.

Although microchipping is still

Make sure your Bichon is well identified with ID tags.

a convenient and practical means of permanent identification, owners must request at the time of insertion a chip that is going to keep up with technological changes and that is currently able to be read or detected by the majority of scanners. The best bet for safe identification of your Bichon is to use a dual system: ID tags and either a tattoo or microchip. Whichever you choose, remember to register your contact information and update it if your address or phone number changes.

TRAVEL

One of the best things about your new Bichon is that you'll find him perfectly portable. Here are some tips on how to travel with your new best friend.

Coming Home

You've picked out your perfect Bichon. You've bought everything imaginable to make your new companion happy in his new home. Now it's time to go get him and bring him to your house. To do that, you'll also need to make some preparation for his trip.

It's a good idea to carry a bag of dog-related supplies with you. Consider packing:

- Thermos or bottled water, water bowl, healthy treats or a small serving of what his regular food will be
- Paper towels, carpet cleaner, sandwich bags (for solid messes),

If you prepare in advance, your Bichon's trip home should be problem free.

plastic bags for disposing of soiled towels or pooper-scooper bags, waterless shampoo (rinse-free) for emergency cleanup if puppy gets carsick and vomits on himself, air freshener spray
- Extra lead and puppy collar, blanket, and chew toy for crate.

When planning your trip, pick routes that aren't too winding, hilly, or bumpy and which could cause your puppy to get carsick. For safety, transport the puppy in his crate. Place the crate where it will not slide or fall while the vehicle is in motion. If you have a long journey, allow time for toilet breaks. Make sure that your Bichon's lead is securely fastened before you open the car doors and get him out, and exercise him in an area away from traffic.

Ideally, travel with a family member or friend who can help you transport your new puppy. That way, when you need to stop for a break, you won't have to leave your Bichon alone in the car, where he could become overheated, chilled, or anxious.

Down the Road

Bichons travel well. They enjoy being with you, and they enjoy going to meet new people, see new places, and maybe meet new Bichon friends as well.

- Start by getting your dog used to travelling in the car. Begin with short rides, maybe just around the block, then step up to a trip to the park, then an all-day expedition, before venturing out on an overnight trip.
- If you are going on holiday, take your dog to the vet for a pre-trip check up. If necessary, purchase a sufficient quantity of any medications your pet will need while you're away. A small supply of travel sickness pills might come in handy, just in case. It is a good idea to locate a vet at your holiday destination in case of emergencies.
- Plan and organise your trip. Before you make reservations at a hotel or bed and breakfast, find out if pets are welcome. Make a list of items to pack, including your dog's supplies. Have written instructions and permission forms for your dog's care should you be incapacitated or injured.
- Keep your dog confined or restrained during travel. In an accident, a loose dog can become lost, seriously injured, or even killed. Secure a crate into a seat or baggage area and place your dog in the crate. If crating is not possible, buckle him into a pet seatbelt harness.
- Put home and temporary travel identification tags on your dog in case he does get away. Temporary tags should contain your mobile phone

number, a local phone if applicable, and should be updated for every change in location. If your pet is microchipped or tattooed, keep a copy of the registration numbers with you when you travel. It's a good idea to place a colour photo of your pet with these papers.

• Take your dog's usual food with you. Don't switch brands while travelling because this could cause digestive distress. Store food in sealed containers that prevent spoilage. Feed your dog at his usual times, using nonbreakable or disposable bowls.

• Don't feed or give your dog a large quantity of water 1 to 2 hours prior to travel. While en route, stop about every 3 hours so that your dog can relieve himself, stretch his legs, and get a drink.

• Always scoop the poop! Be courteous to others and clean up after your pet. Carry pick-up bags to remove faeces and only allow your dog to relieve himself in designated pet exercise areas.

• Maintain your dog's normal activity level. He'll sleep more soundly at night and be more relaxed during the day.

• Teach your dog travelling manners. Don't let him disturb other travellers.

Travelling with your Bichon requires some extra work, but most owners feel it's worth the effort.

Bad Travellers

It is very rare for a Bichon to be a bad traveller, but it can happen. The most common problems are travel sickness, or a dog that refuses to settle.

If your Bichon is car-sick, observe the following precautions:

• Leave at least 2 hours between feeding your Bichon and going in the car.

• Restrict access to water 1 hour before a journey.

• Confine your Bichon in a crate or a travel harness so movement is limited.

• It may help if your Bichon cannot see out of the car window, as this can induce nausea.

The vet will prescribe travel sickness tablets, or you can try a natural remedy which may help. Ginger and Peppermint are both effective in treating travel sickness, or you can buy a specially formulated natural remedy which contains a number of herbal ingredients.

If your Bichon refuses to settle, try the following:

• Turn on the CD player—hopefully he won't try to compete with the noise!

- Sit in the car with your Bichon for short periods with the engine turned off so there is no 'trigger' for barking or over excitement.
- Go on short trips with a reward, such a play in the park. In this way, your Bichon will associate the car with good things.

LEAVING YOUR BICHON BEHIND

Not all trips will be suitable for taking your Bichon along. When you have to leave your dog behind, you can board him in a kennel or have a petsitter come into your home. Ask several vital questions of any kennel or petsitter before choosing the one who will take care of your dog while you're away. Make sure that the facility or sitter is reliable and informed. Also make certain that your Bichon does not suffer from separation anxiety before leaving him (more information in Chapter 6).

If you can't take your Bichon with you, a kennel or petsitter may be the answer.

Boarding

A boarding kennel might be a good option for your Bichon.

How To Find a Kennel

Begin your search by checking with other dog-owning friends and neighbours who travel without their canine. Are they happy with the kennel they use? Talk to them about the facilities and care that is provided. Your vet may be able to make a recommendation.

Look up listings in the yellow pages. For convenience, check with those kennels that are located near your home or business first. Set up appointments to visit their facilities and meet the staff who will be caring for your dog. Ask the owner or manager for references.

What To Look For in a Kennel

When you arrive, get a tour of the kenneling and exercise areas. If a tour is refused, this may be a warning not to board your dog

Online Help

Two organisations that can help you locate sitters in your area are www.dogservices.co.uk and www.ukpetsitter.com.

there. On your tour, look for or ask the following:

- Is the facility clean, including kennels, crates, runs, and yard areas?
- Are outside views or runs provided? Is the building safe from fire hazards?
- How frequently are the kennels, crates and runs cleaned?
- How often are the dogs taken out for exercise and toilet breaks?
- Do the dogs have fresh water?
- Does the staff truly like and understand animals, and are they attentive to them?
- Are they willing to accommodate your dog's special needs?
- Will they administer your dog's daily medication or feed the same diet given at home?
- Is your dog permitted to keep toys in his run?

Discuss the kennel's policies. Most require that all animals are up to date with their vaccinations. What type of proof of vaccination will you need to provide? What does the kennel do in case of a medical emergency involving your dog? Are their rates competitive with other kennels, and do they reflect the quality of the care given? Is payment due before you leave or when you return? Do some services cost extra? Get a schedule of their hours and times when you can drop off and pick up your dog.

Once you select a kennel, give them detailed, written care instructions for your dog. Leave your travel itinerary, along with phone numbers where they can contact you in the event of an emergency. If permitted, send your dog's favourite toy and bedding to the kennel. You may want to leave one of your unlaundered shirts with your dog—an item that has your scent and smells like home. This will comfort your Bichon while you're away from him, and remind him that you will return.

Petsitters

Many Bichons are happier staying at home, in familiar surroundings. If this is the best choice for your dog, you must find a reliable, qualified petsitter.

There are national organisations that can help you locate sitters in your area. Check their websites at www.dogservices.co.uk and www.ukpetsitter.com. You should also check with your dog-owning friends to see which petsitting services they have used.

Because a sitter will come into your home and have sole care of your dog, ask for multiple references. Sitters should be fully registered and insured. Anyone can call themselves a petsitter, but only the best ones for your dogs will meet these requirements.

Before a petsitter comes to your home, you will be asked to provide a thorough history of your Bichon's health and habits. It's easier for the sitter—and therefore for your dog—if you leave all of his care items, such as bowls, medicines, and lead, in a central location. Provide a sufficient quantity of food for more days than you plan to be gone.

Just as you would for a kennel, write down all specific care instructions and a breakdown of your travel plans and contact numbers. Furnish any information the sitter will need in order to be safe in your house, and contact numbers in case of emergencies.

Rates for petsitters vary by area, but can run about one-and-a-half times per visit what you might pay per day at a kennel. The advantages your dog gets for the extra expense may be well worth the difference. Your dog will be in familiar surroundings and able to sleep in his own bed and play with his own toys. He'll be fed the same foods at the same times as normal, get to walk or exercise as usual and, if he needs medications, they can be administered just as you would give them. Although he'll still be alone many hours, the attention he receives will be personal and the sitter can reassure your Bichon that you will soon return.

Finding someone or someplace you trust to look after your Bichon will help give you peace of mind.

Home Boarding

Another option is to take your Bichon to a family that specialise in boarding a limited number of small dogs in their home. Although your dog is away from his home, he is still in a house with people who are there at least as much as you normally would be with him. Home boarding services match reservations by age, health, and temperament so that your dog is only with other dogs with whom he is compatible. Your dog will also be maintained on his normal diet and exercise routine. Fees range between the cost of boarding and petsitting.

You can find home boarders online or in the Yellow Pages. Schedule an appointment to see the home and meet the owners. Ask the same questions you would of a kennel or petsitter, including references. Be prepared to leave the same detailed history and instructions as you would for other services.

Because Bichons are such comfort-loving, people-dependent dogs, home boarding may prove the ideal place to leave your dog when you travel.

Doggy Daycare

If you work long hours, are going to be away just during the days, or if your Bichon needs companionship while you're out and about, you can make an on-going arrangement with a petsitter or a home boarder. In the USA, doggy day care

centres have sprung up, which provide exercise, recreation and companionship for dogs while owners are absent.

In the UK, services on a daily basis are usually provided by petsitters who will come to your home, and will also exercise your dog. Some home boarders offer day care. If you are working, and your Bichon has to be left for long periods – such as four hours at a time—you should make arrangement—so your Bichon has the care and companionship that is essential for this breed.

Check that your dog is happy to mix with other dogs before you consider home boarding.

4

FEEDING

Your Bichon Frise

The expression "you are what you eat" has been repeated so many times that when someone hears it, their eyes glaze over and they tune out any dietary information that follows. But as tired clichés go, this one is worth heeding. For a breed with so many health conditions that can be aggravated by or related to food, the foundation of physical wellbeing and the prevention of problems may rest primarily on solid nutrition. (For an explanation of health conditions in the Bichon that can be affected by diet, see Chapter 8.)

READY TO GO

About 10 years ago, it was estimated that nearly 95 percent of owners fed their dogs pre-prepared dog-food products. While that number may have declined in recent years, due to owners who have started making their dog's food themselves, in order to control the quality of ingredients or provide a specific diet, it is still likely that the huge majority of owners feed their dog a food that they have purchased ready-made.

The Food-Sensitive Bichon

Bichons with allergies or food sensitivities may have fewer problems if ingredients like corn or soybean meal, rice, and meat products of an unnamed meat source are avoided.

Complete Food

Complete dry food diets are by far the most popular choice of dog food. Literally dozens and dozens of brands are available, and many varieties exist within these brands. So, how's an owner supposed to choose? By learning about ingredients and understanding those that are best for your dog.

Ingredients

In the early days, when commercial dry dog foods first became available, these foods served two purposes: to make it more convenient for owners to feed their dogs; and to provide an additional market for grain millers and meat packers to sell the remains or leftover parts that could not be utilised for human consumption.

As people have become more conscious of nutritional health for their dogs, the quality of ingredients in dry food has improved over the years. Many products offer only ingredients that are also suitable for human consumption. But just as many dry foods still exist on the market that use discarded grains and meats as their staple. Some of these items can be used to produce corn or soybean meal, rice mill by-products, wheat mill run, animal digest, and meat by-products of an unnamed meat source; these can be added as a main ingredient to dog food.

Dogs with allergies or food sensitivities may have fewer problems if these types of ingredients are avoided. And, in products where the whole or healthier parts of meat and grain are used, because more, complete nutrients are available in a more digestible, absorbable form,

A dry 'complete' diet is by far the most popular choice of dog food.

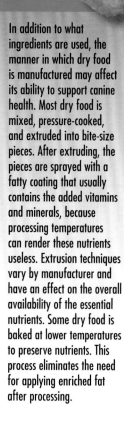

the health of dogs eating these foods should be better.

Other ingredients that add no value to dog food and, in some instances may aggravate or contribute to the development of health problems, include salt, sugars, and artificial preservatives. Propionic acid or hydrochloric acid may also be added to less digestible forms of grain foods in an effort to make them more digestible.

The meat used in dog food is another area in which a great deal of variation occurs from one manufacturer to the next. Main meats include chicken, beef, lamb, fish, turkey, and their by-products, plus some specialty meats like venison. Additional ingredients are the grain base that holds the product together as well as a large variety of vegetables and even fruits or herbs. Sources for these products differ as much as the flavour does.

Before you make a selection, learn what the terminology on dry dog food means and choose the healthiest for your Bichon. Healthy dry food does not equate with tasteless. Pick a meat that supports your dog's health needs or supports any special diet that he must follow, related to any medical conditions he might have. If your Bichon has allergies or urinary stones, be cautious about secondary ingredients, like vegetables, until you are certain which ones are safe for him.

In most cases complete diets are formulated for different needs, depending on the dog's age and lifestyle. There are complete diets for puppies, diets for nursing bitches, diets for ageing dogs, and even diets for obese dogs that need to shed the pounds.

Making Changes

For the majority of owners who choose to feed a complete diet, it should be considered as *complete*, i.e. requiring no additional supplements. Most vets and other dog experts recommend that, once a diet is selected, it should not be changed continually and that, when it must be changed, it should be done so gradually.

In the case of a Bichon who is allergic, this may not always work. Repeated exposure to an ingredient can sensitise a dog to the point where the ingredient becomes an allergen. By rotating foods, this problem can be avoided, and finicky eaters may be appeased by the variety. However, if your Bichon is on a diet specifically geared for a health condition, or if he suffers from digestive disorders where changes may result in a flare-up of symptoms, do not rotate his diet without first consulting your vet.

How's It Made?

In addition to what ingredients are used, the manner in which dry food is manufactured may affect its ability to support canine health. Most dry food is mixed, pressure-cooked, and extruded into bite-size pieces. After extruding, the pieces are sprayed with a fatty coating that usually contains the added vitamins and minerals, because processing temperatures can render these nutrients useless. Extrusion techniques vary by manufacturer and have an effect on the overall availability of the essential nutrients. Some dry food is baked at lower temperatures to preserve nutrients. This process eliminates the need for applying enriched fat after processing.

Semi-moist Food

These foods are normally packaged to look like hamburger patties or chunks of fresh beef. While they may have an appealing look sitting on the grocery store shelf, their appearance goes unnoticed by a dog. Semi-moist foods are conveniently packaged and have a long shelf life, but they are loaded with artificial preservatives, artificial colours, and artificial flavours.

Propylene glycol, one of the prime additives in some semi-moist foods or treats, is a mostly tasteless, gooey liquid used in the manufacturing of de-icing agents and polyester compounds, and as a solvent for plastic and paints. However, it is permitted to be used in foods, where it is utilised as a solvent for flavouring and colouring. It is allowed to retain moisture in a food product.

Although propylene glycol is recognised as being safe to use in food, research has been carried out which may cause some concern to dog owners. It has been discovered that propylene glycol can increase the amount of acid in the body, which, in large quantities, might cause metabolic problems.

Besides a cocktail of additives, semi-moist food is also high in sugars in the form of fructose, corn syrup, and sucrose. It can be a source of hidden sodium as well. For the Bichon who is prone to bladder stones, diabetes, dental disease, or digestive disorders, adding salt, sugar, or acid-causing humectants to his diet may not be a prudent choice. Think very carefully before selecting semi-moist food as the main component of your Bichon's diet.

Canned dog food is very high in moisture content.

Canned Food

Also known as soft or moist food, canned dog food is very high in moisture content. Between 70 to 85 percent of the ingredients may come from water, broth, or a combination of both. Meats of many varieties are the next main ingredient. Vegetables, potatoes, whole or partial grains, and even fruit can be added to the mixture. Vitamins, minerals, and sometimes amino acids are also added as needed in order to provide essential nutrients.

Because the process of canning a product is a means of preserving a product, it is seldom necessary to add synthetic preservatives. However, check the label closely for brands that add preservatives or artificial flavour enhancers. Ingredients in some canned foods that your dog would be better off without include salts and sodiums like sodium tripolyphosphate, sodium alginate, and chlorine chloride; soy products like flour or soybean meal; colours or brighteners, like yellow #5 or titanium dioxide; and flavours that may not be safe for dogs, such as onion powder.

Feeding a portion of canned food with dry food is a good way to get finicky eaters "primed" and ready to eat their dry meal. It's also an excellent method of increasing water intake for Bichons prone to stone formation. Canned food can be used to make up about 20 to 25 percent of your Bichon's diet.

Most dogs enjoy the flavour of canned food. When feeding canned, be careful to pick a meat source of high quality and one that is not an allergen for your dog. Avoid brands with salts and other unnecessary additives, and those that use a low grade of meat. Canned food tends to be higher in calories and not as healthy for teeth as dry food, so don't overfeed—a little goes a long way.

Dry + Canned

You can feed your Bichon a combination of dry food and canned food, which is an excellent method for increasing water intake in stone prone dogs.

BUYING A BALANCED FOOD

Most owners prefer the convenience of buying ready-prepared dog foods, rather than preparing home-cooked balanced meals, so it is important to understand exactly what you are buying.

All commercial dog foods should meet a minimum nutritional requirement. In the UK, pet food is controlled by the Food Standards Agency (FSA), which has to adhere to EC guidelines. Pet food manufacturers also belong to the Pet Food Manufacturer's Association (PFMA), which, in turn, follows guidelines laid down by the European Pet Food Industry Federation (FEDIAF).

One of the biggest favours you can do for your Bichon is to read the label of ingredients on dog food before buying it. But reading it isn't enough; you need to understand what each ingredient is, what the source of the ingredient might be, and what the possible long-term health consequences could be of consuming some substances on a regular basis.

DOG FOOD DECONSTRUCTED

The information that is detailed on a food label follows guidelines

Did You Know?

Nutrition is the process of absorbing and utilising nutrients in a manner that promotes wellness and supports the body and its functions.

given by the Food Standards Agency, working with the Pet Food Manufacturer's Association. Every label contains the following:

- **Typical Analysis.** The percentage of the following must be listed: proteins, oils and fats, fibre, moisture (when it exceeds 14 per cent), ash (this represents the mineral content of the food and is determined by the burning of the product).
- **Ingredients List.** The ingredients must be listed in descending order by weight. They can be indicated using category names laid down by the Regulations (e.g. 'meat and animal derivatives', 'derivatives of vegetable origin'). Alternatively, ingredients can be listed by individual names. When an ingredient is used that does not fall into any of the prescribed categories, its individual name must be listed. In all other circumstances, mixing individual names and category names is not permitted. If particular attention is drawn to a specific ingredient (e.g. With Chicken), the percentage of that ingredient component must also be listed.
- **Additives.** If preservatives, antioxidants or colourants have been added to the product their presence has to be declared using category or chemical names, in accordance with the Feeding Stuffs Regulations.
- **Vitamins.** If Vitamins A, D and E are added to the product, their presence and level has to be declared. The level must include both the quantity naturally present in the raw materials and the quantity added. The Regulations also lay down the units that must be used to declare the level.
- **Best Before Date.** This date indicates the minimum storage life of the product. The month and year must be shown.
- **Bar Code.** This is not a legal requirement but allows for information about sales, stocks, etc.
- **Batch Number.** A batch number or the date of manufacture must be given to facilitate traceability of the product. This may be given either in the statutory statement or elsewhere on the package/label/container, in which case the statutory statement shall indicate where it can be found.
- **Net Weight.** The net weight must be given in accordance with the Feeding Stuffs Rgulations 2002. The Weights and Measures (Packaged Goods) Regulations 1986 lays down the exact marking and size of lettering required. The net weight may be given either in the Statutory Statement or elsewhere on the packaging/label, in which case the Statutory Statement should indicate where it may be found.
- **Name and Address.** This is the name and address of the company responsible for the products. It may be a manufacturer, packer, importer, seller or distributor.

Ingredients

In order to understand the ingredients included in diets it is worth looking in more detail at some that are commonly listed.

- **Meat.** Meat is designated to mean the skeletal muscle tissue, as well as the tongue, heart, oesophagus, or diaphragm of cattle, chicken, turkey, or lamb. It may or may not include skin, sinew, or the blood vessels that can be found in these tissues. It is to exclude feet, hair, heads, entrails, feathers, and such. *Meat and bone meal* is the processed product derived from meat parts and also includes processed bone.

- **Cereal.** Cereal and other grains used in the production of dog food, which can include rice, wheat, barley, oats, corn, soy, and others. Dogs with allergies may have fewer problems if they are not fed foods containing soy, corn, or wheat. Grains may be ground or whole, and are usually noted as such. Grain parts can include bran, hulls (the coarse outer parts), germ, and germ meal, which is the inner part of the grain kernel normally processed to remove the oil. *Grain meal*, especially soybean meal, may be processed mechanically, but it may also be de-hulled using chemical solvents.

- **Beet Pulp.** The residue from dried sugar beets, left after the sugar portion is removed and dried. It is an insoluble fibre and is moderately fermentable. It is usually added to dog food to "compact stool" for easier owner clean-up. Beet pulp may provide necessary fibre and promote the growth of beneficial intestinal bacteria. But in some dogs, it can cause the cells that absorb and break down nutrients to function improperly, thus depriving the dog's body of necessary nutrients and allowing bacterial overgrowth.

Beet Pulp

In the Bichon, beet pulp can be related to problems with tear staining and allergies.

- **By-products.** By-products are the unprocessed parts that remain after the muscle meat has been removed, including blood, bone, brains, intestines (emptied), kidneys, livers, lungs, spleen, stomach, and some fatty tissues. It should exclude hair, hooves, horn, and teeth. *By-product meal* is made from the processed (rendered)

Before feeding your Bichon any prepared food, learn how to read the label.

Find Out More

If you want more information about a particular diet, call or email the manufacturer. Contact details are usually on the label.

parts. Poultry by-product meal may include the use of feet, intestines, necks, and undeveloped eggs, but excludes feathers and heads.

- **Animal Digest.** The material remaining after a process of cleaning, boiling, and separating (sometimes with chemical enzymes) the otherwise unused portions of an animal. It is used as a meat source in dog food. Digest excludes hair, horns, hooves, teeth, and feathers.
- **Additive.** An additive is a substance added to food during processing to preserve colour or flavour, or to stabilise the ingredients; nutrients may also be considered additives if they do not naturally occur in a food product and are added during processing to make a food nutritious.
- **Artificial.** The word *artificial* on the label means it has been manufactured; it is a substance that does not occur naturally.
- **Natural.** *Natural* means a substance derived from an animal or vegetable origin, as opposed to manufactured chemicals. It denotes a food product containing no chemical additives.
- **Organic.** Organic substances are derived from living organisms. It may also indicate that the ingredient was produced from a plant or animal source where no chemicals were used, such as pesticides, growth hormones, and so forth.
- **Preservative.** A preservative is a chemical substance that prevents decomposition or fermentation in food; it may be natural or artificial in origin.

PET FOOD PRICES

The prices of pet food are as varied as the choices. Just as in any other item that a shopper purchases, the price normally is determined by the quality of the item and the effort required to produce that level of quality.

In recent years, stories have circulated the Internet about the horrible, unspeakable "things" that are put into pet food. Some are urban myths, others are exaggerations and, sadly, some are true. It is important when choosing which food to feed your dog that you understand what the sources are for the ingredients in your dog's food.

Feeding the best foods to your Bichon is the foundation of good health.

When an animal is slaughtered for human consumption, a large portion of the carcass and organs remain. These leftovers are used as the meat source for pet food. Not necessarily a bad thing, as dogs in the wild normally would eat these parts; it's just necessary to ascertain that a sufficient quantity of protein and vitamins are also available.

As mentioned earlier, a label will not necessarily note the source of the meat, so how do you detect whether it contains all the nutrients your pet needs? The price will be very low, and the product label will contain mostly categories, rather than naming all the individual ingredients. Dog foods marketed with ingredient lists that contain only vague category names do so because this allows manufacturers to change the ingredients without changing the labelling. Manufacturers are constantly on the lookout for cheap ingredients and it is more profitable to purchase whatever happens to be available than to stick to the same recipe regardless of cost. It is worth bearing in mind that protein obtained from high-quality meat sources is far more expensive than protein sourced from soy, for example.

You do not have to spend a fortune on dog food made with 100 per cent chicken breast to feed your Bichon a high-quality diet. However, you get what you pay for, so avoid very cheap products and make sure you understand the information on the previous pages. Also be guided by your sense of smell. Poor-quality food often has a strong or unappealing odour that is often masked by fatty sprays designed to make the food taste better to a dog.

The role of diet and its effects on general health has become better understood in recent years. There is also evidence to suggest that poor-quality dog food can affect toy breeds, such as the Bichon, more than larger breeds. As your Bichon's guardian you are responsible for feeding him a diet that will ensure he thrives.

A Healthy Diet

To remain fit and healthy, a Bichon must be fed a diet that is suitable for its needs. Ask your Bichon's breeder for advice, as in most cases a breeder can draw on years of specialist experience.

Watch the Fat

The fats with which dry food is usually sprayed may be another area where the source of origin is a potential problem. Because no prohibitions exist against doing so, some manufacturers may buy leftover, used grease from the restaurant and food-preparation industries. Again, this will not be noted on the label, but can be suspected if the fat sources have long, inexplicable names and if the price on the food is low.

MAKING IT YOURSELF

You may decide to forgo the commercial dog-food route and prepare your Bichon's food yourself. Home-prepared and raw diets have become increasingly popular and, with a little research, time, and effort, you can provide your Bichon with a healthy diet made lovingly by your own hands.

Home-Prepared Dog Foods

Very low-priced food is not a good deal for your Bichon's health.

With recent health trends in food, some owners are now preparing their dog's food instead of buying it. Many reasons exist to do this: to make your dog feel special, supply human-quality foods you purchase yourself, meet the needs of a special diet, or avoid problem ingredients for an allergic or stone-forming Bichon. This can be done as simply as adding an extra portion to the—healthy!—meals you make for the rest of your family. Alternatively, you can be as elaborate as buying doggy cookbooks and separate ingredients, and selecting multiple daily dishes for your dog alone.

Before embarking on a canine culinary venture, you must gain some knowledge about canine nutrition. Read books that provide you not only with recipes, but with a nutritional analysis of the recipes and information on basic nutrition, particularly as it pertains to dogs. If you prefer to concoct your own special blends, consider consulting a veterinary nutritionist about what and how much you plan to feed your Bichon.

What Is Protien?

Proteins are composed of amino acids. They are the basic elements that comprise the essential material of all cells. They are the building blocks of the body, used for muscles, organs, enzymes, hormones, and the immune system. Protein is the least readily available form of energy, and is used primarily for building and maintaining the body.

Ingredients

Choosing ingredients for your dog's homemade meals require understanding his personal health concerns as well as his taste buds. In most cases, low sodium or salt, no or low sugar, and the avoidance of excess fats is best. Protein in the form of meat, eggs, or possibly dairy products (beware of dairy products in allergic or stone-forming Bichons) should constitute between 10 and 30 percent of your dog's diet; carbohydrates, including fibre, about 25 to 45 percent; and fat, an essential nutrient, the remainder.

Meat sources can be any lean cut that your Bichon likes and to which he is not allergic. Possible choices are chicken, turkey, lamb, fish, venison, sometimes beef, and organ meats like liver, kidneys, or heart. Sufficient fat may be present in the meat source so that no additional fat is required. If you need to add fat, use oils like olive or sunflower, but stay away from corn or soy oils since corn and soy may be allergens to many Bichons.

Carbohydrates should come from cereals like rice, oats, barley, and sometimes wheat if your dog is not allergic. A nearly endless variety of vegetables and fruits, which are complex carbohydrates, should be included. Avoid onions, raisins, grapes, and some nuts like almonds and macadamia, which are purported to cause serious illness in some dogs. You may also wish to exclude veggies that can ferment and cause flatulence, like cabbage.

Herbs commonly used to flavour cooked dishes may also be used in your dog's recipes, but use sparingly. Vary what you feed. Unlike recommendations with purchased, dry dog food, homemade doggy meals can and should rotate their ingredients, unless you have been instructed otherwise by your vet.

Cook your dog's meals with the same precautions you use when handling food for human consumption. Store unused portions in the refrigerator, and discard any that remains uneaten after about 3 days.

Making the Switch

Home-cooked dog food can be used as an additive to dry food, or as the entire diet. If you are switching your dog to food that is entirely home prepared, do so gradually. Watch your dog for any signs of problems that may be brewing. How are his bowel and bladder habits? Do the urine and stool look normal or okay? Is he showing any symptoms of gastric distress—flatulence, vomiting, grass-eating? Is he lethargic, or is he eating less?

In a few weeks, see how your dog's coat and skin look. Are allergies better? Does the fur shine? Does your dog have more energy? Does he act like he feels better? If so, you're probably on the right track. Just make sure to communicate with your vet on a regular basis about your Bichon's health if you are feeding a home-cooked diet.

Pet Food Pricing

The bottom line on pet food pricing: If it's bargain-basement priced, the food is not a good deal for your dog. Beware of the opposite side of this coin: Just because a dog food carries a hefty price tag does not guarantee that it will be an extremely healthy, nutritious food for your dog. Check consumer reviews and ask other Bichon owners if their dog does well on certain brands. Premium-grade foods will be higher priced but in the long run, your dog will get what you pay for in improved nutrition and better health.

Fish is often used in allergy-elimination diets.

Raw Diets

The ultimate trend in home-prepared food is to feed raw. Sometimes known as BARF, which stands for Biologically Appropriate Raw Foods, this special raw diet is meant to mimic the foods that a dog would eat naturally in the wild. The theory behind feeding this primal dog fare is that it is the type of food a dog's system was made to digest, and thus it provides nutrition that results in the greatest levels of health.

Raw meal recipes are based on combining about 60 to 70 percent raw meat and about 30 to 40 percent vegetables. Meats used are usually chicken, beef, or lamb, obtained fresh from a butcher and prepared by home chunking or grinding on the day of preparation. Vegetables can be whatever your dog likes, also purchased fresh, and ground in with the meat. If your dog is not allergic, cereal carbohydrates like barley, oats, rice, or pasta can be added, as can some fruits. Bones are normally included in the BARF diet, also in the raw form.

The thought of feeding raw may make some owners' stomachs turn, particularly for those who have experienced a case of food poisoning. Raw meat harbours greater numbers of disease-inducing bacteria than does cooked meat. But dogs, with their shorter intestinal tracts and more acidic stomachs, are less likely to be affected adversely by *E. coli* or *Salmonella*.

Still, feeding raw requires that the meat source be fresh and clean, and that is it safely handled and processed. Some sources suggest freezing the meat before preparing the meals (thaw only in the refrigerator, never at room temperature), and others suggest a quick dip in boiling water, or a rinse with grapefruit seed extract to reduce or kill bacteria. Once prepared, raw meals must be frozen. Like meats for human consumption, shelf life is limited, so date the package before storing and discard after the expiration of safety. The meals ready to use should be thawed in the refrigerator, where they should never be stored longer than 2 days.

Carb Facts

Carbohydrates include starches and sugars, which are broken down and quickly utilised, and are a source of ready energy; they may also include fibre. Carbs are either simple, those which break down more easily and are more rapidly absorbed; or complex, those which require more digestive processes to break down, and that take slightly longer to be absorbed.

Feeding bones also carries risks. Although uncooked bones are softer and less likely to splinter, the possibility still exists for bone fragments to become lodged in or perforate the mouth, oesophagus, stomach, or intestines. Such obstructions or perforations require medical attention, often emergency surgery, and can result in death. Because of their small size, when feeding raw bones to the Bichon, it is recommended that they be ground as part of the meat and vegetable mixture.

Preparing raw meals can be a rather complicated process that involves frequent shopping for ingredients; the purchase of grinders, knives, cutting boards, and storage containers for making the meals; and extensive precautions in handling the raw meat, followed by cleaning the prep items and surfaces areas. Several dog food manufacturers offer a foundation product meant not only to provide a complete and balanced raw diet, but to help reduce the amount of effort needed to prepare raw foods. These products come frozen, and owners can serve as-is or add a few ingredients to complete.

Health Risks

Feeding raw meats can pose serious risks to animal and human health. Gastroenteritis, amoebic intestinal infection, nausea, vomiting, diarrhoea, dehydration, and even death can ensue if meat is contaminated with enough bacteria. Dogs can become carriers of some bacterial gastrointestinal diseases without being infected, which can pose a risk to other animals and humans in the household. If you're going to feed a raw diet to your dog, be extremely cautious in your purchases and preparations, and remain alert for any symptoms of gastrointestinal illness.

Health Benefits

Despite the risks and involved preparation, for some dogs, BARF diets may be the route to optimum health. Some owners swear by a raw diet for Bichons with allergies and other health conditions. Before starting your dog on BARF, consult with your vet; dogs with certain health problems must have their diet more strictly regulated.

Make the switch gradually, over a period of at least 7 to 10 days, beginning with small portions. Monitor your dog's health during

Foods To Avoid

Avoid giving your Bichon the following foods:

- Alcoholic beverages
- Almonds
- Cat food
- Chocolate
- Coffee
- Cooked bones that may splinter
- Fatty, greasy foods, or butter
- Grapes
- Human vitamins
- Macadamia nuts
- Onions
- Raisins
- Scraps or leftovers you wouldn't eat
- Tea

If your Bichon is one of those who suffers from calcium oxalate stones, additional foods may also be forbidden.

Some owners have found that a raw diet can help Bichons who have food allergies.

the trial period and determine if raw is best for him. With the proper nutrient balance, raw can be fed either a few times a week, or for all meals.

TIME FOR DINNER

Just like humans, dogs need regular meal times. Bichons are creatures of habit, and most prefer to be fed at the same time every day. This need should be accommodated whenever possible. But also teach your dog that a little flexibility in feeding schedules is acceptable. Since daily life is not always predictable, a dog who can adapt to small changes in his meal times will be less stressed when you are delayed in getting his food in front of him. How often you feed your dog will depend on his age.

Puppies

Puppies need to eat frequently. They have smaller stomachs that fill more quickly, and they need to consume more calories because of their increased energy levels. Nutrients to support their growing bodies are needed at more frequent intervals as well.

How Often?

Until around the age of 3 to 4 months, puppies should be fed four times daily. After that, reduce feedings to three times daily, until they are about their full height. This typically occurs between 8 and 10 months of age. Once a puppy is full grown, he can be switched to an adult schedule.

How Much?

Although pups need more food, they should not be overfed. Growing Bichons should get about 236 ml of food daily, separated into however many portions they need based on age—59 ml for four feedings, 78 ml for three. Be guided by your puppy's activity level and weight when adjusting the total quantity of food served.

When feeding four times daily, try to space the meals about three to four hours apart over a period of 13 to 16 hours, with the first meal being served upon rising and the last about an hour or slightly more before bedtime.

Choosing a Puppy Food

Choose a puppy food using the same guidelines as for any other dog food. Ask the advice of your breeder. On what food have her puppies thrived? If you're going to change brands when you bring your pup home, do so gradually over at least 3 days, by mixing in a little of the new food with the old, until you are no longer serving the original food.

Pups can usually be switched to an adult food between the ages of 7 to 9 months. Some lines of premium dog foods provide nutrition of sufficient quality in their products that they do not offer a separate "puppy" food. These foods have enough nutrients in the proper ratio and quantities that the additional daily feedings provide the extra calories and nutrients needed by a puppy. Choose the type that gives your puppy the maximum health value.

Nutritional Terms

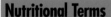

Amino acids. The organic building blocks for protein; the "essential amino acids" cannot be made by the body and must be obtained from the diet.

Balanced. A food in which the nutrients occur in the proper ratio to one another.

Calorie, Kcal. A unit of heat; used to express the energy value of food; this information is used to determine feeding directions. Dog food is calculated by "kcals," which means kilocalories of metabolisable energy per kilogramme of food.

Chelated minerals. A chemical process by which minerals are structurally changed into a more digestible form for better absorption.

Chemical. A substance composed of various processed chemicals; chemicals occur naturally or may be manufactured.

Complete. Contains the nutrients essential to maintain life and basic health.

Enriched. Has vitamins and minerals added after cooking or processing.

Fatty Acids (FA). A subcomponent of fat. Some FAs, known as the "essential fatty acids," cannot be synthesised

in the body and must be obtained in the diet. Examples of these are omega-6, omega-3, and linoleic acids; both the amount and ratio of FAs consumed are nutritionally important to skin and fur.

Fibre. A form of partially or wholly indigestible carbohydrates found in plants. Fibre can be fermentable or nonfermentable. Fermentable fibre is broken down into some fatty acids; nonfermentable fibre provides bulk. A moderately fermentable fibre helps maintain stool fluid content and movement through the intestines.

Metabolism. The workings of the physical and chemical processes in the body, especially related to digestion and utilisation of nutrients. It is the process by which energy is made available to the body.

Minerals. Nonorganic substances, minerals are components of the skeletal structure and are essential for normal nerve conduction and fluid balance in the body.

Nutrient. Nourishing substances that must be provided by food, or as a component of food, since it cannot be synthesised by the body. Essential nutrients include proteins, carbohydrates, fat, vitamins, and minerals. They are necessary for growth and to maintain normal life functions.

Puppies need to consume more calories because of their increased energy levels.

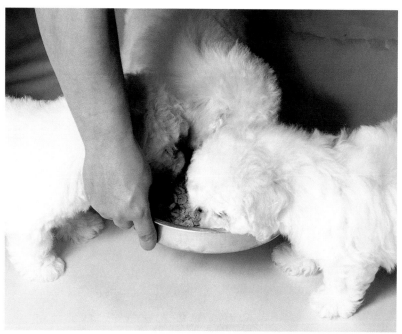

Adult Dogs

Although not fully grown or mature, when it comes to food, your Bichon should be considered an adult and ready for regular food by the age of 7 or 9 months. Adulthood won't be completely reached until your dog is somewhere around 18 to 24 months of age, but puppy food is too rich and too high in some nutrients (such as calcium), for a dog who is no longer a young, rapidly growing puppy.

How Often?

It used to be suggested that adult dogs should be fed once daily, but this thinking has changed. Most Bichons do better if they are fed twice daily throughout their adult life. This can prevent vomiting of pale yellow foam from a too-empty stomach, as well as eating too quickly when meal time finally arrives.

Feeding times for the adult Bichon should be twice daily, once in the morning and once in the evening. Try to space these meals about 12 hours apart.

How Much?

Unless your dog is very active, a 118 ml to 142 ml total of premium dry food daily is generally ample to maintain ideal body weight. Some Bichons may need as much as a full cup per day. Dogs who compete and train on a regular basis will probably require more calories and protein, and may need more food, or to be fed a product that is higher in protein and fat.

Veterans

As any dog ages, his metabolism slows. Energy and activity levels also drop. Some older dogs may develop a tendency to gain weight at this point, while others can actually become too thin. The age at which this happens varies from dog to dog. Generally, dogs are considered to be veterans at around 7 years old, but, for the longer-lived Bichon, senior status may be a few more years down the road.

Time for a Veteran Food?

It may be difficult to determine exactly the day you should switch your dog's food to a diet for veterans, so watch for subtle clues that he's slowing down. Results of routine blood tests taken at an annual exam are probably some of the best clues as to when it's time to change the food. Indicators of kidney and liver function, as well as functionality of the digestive tract, are signs that say when, as well as what type of diet your Bichon may need.

For those prone to weight gain, a food that has reduced fat and calories may be needed. Veterans who are underweight will need more calories and possibly more protein. Recent studies have determined that older dogs need more protein to maintain muscle mass and healthy organ functions. Only in a limited number of health conditions, like certain kidney diseases, is it necessary to reduce protein consumption as a dog ages.

As your Bichon grows older, watch for signs that food sensitivities may be developing or increasing as his body starts to function less efficiently. Also watch closely for changes in eating habits that may indicate the beginning of an age-related health problem with the kidneys, liver, pancreas, or other aging organs. Special diets may be needed to compensate for failing health. Ask your vet which is best for your ageing Bichon.

Did You Know?

Vitamins are organic substances found in food; vitamins are an essential component of nutrition. They are necessary in small amounts for normal metabolic processes; however, they do not provide energy nor are they materials used in the building of cells.

How Much?

The amount you feed a veteran dog should not change drastically, possibly a little more or a little less. And you should

Puppies and adults have different nutritional requirements.

still feed at the same times as usual. With a few dogs, a third meal may need to be added back into the schedule, but this should be done on the advice of your vet. An older dog may also lose some sense of taste and smell, which can make food less appealing. Adding tasty but healthy titbits of meat, sodium-free broth, canned food, or soft vegetables may pique interest in a flagging appetite. A healthy and tasty diet is one of the best ways you can show your older Bichon you still care.

Free-Choice Feeding

Leaving dry food in a bowl and available at all times for your dog is a feeding method known as free-choice feeding. This option allows dogs, such as veterans, who may eat slowly or only a little at a time, to nibble, go, and return as they please. It's sometimes a useful alternative for finicky eaters who can't be persuaded to eat an entire meal at a scheduled time.

Free-choice feeding should not be used with Bichons who have a tendency to overeat or gain weight easily. For households with multiple dogs, free-choice feeding may not be a good idea either, because it is difficult to monitor individual food intake. Some dogs may get too much food while others get too little, special diets can't be kept separate, and the dogs may quarrel over the food.

SPECIAL DIETS

If your dog is one of those Bichons who is plagued by allergies,

Taste Tempters

If your older dog seems less interested in his food, try adding tasty but healthy titbits of meat, sodium-free broth, canned food, or soft vegetables to tempt his appetite.

bladder stones, urinary tract infections, diabetes, pancreatitis, or inflammatory bowel disease or, if he develops some other problem like kidney or heart disease, he may need to be placed on a controlled diet of a special prescription food.

A few pet food manufacturers supply a variety of canned and some dry foods made from ingredients aimed directly at preventing some conditions, controlling the symptoms of others, or restricting and balancing certain nutrients in the diet. These foods are available only on the recommendation of and through a vet.

Dogs who require these foods will first have been tested for and diagnosed with a specific condition by a vet. As part of a treatment plan, the appropriate food is prescribed, and a diet plan laid out. These foods may need to be fed for only a period of time, or for the life of your dog. They may be given once or twice a day, sometimes alone or in conjunction with other foods.

While your dog is eating these specially formulated and balanced foods, your vet will also advise you about what regular foods your dog may have, or those foods that he must not be given. Before changing your dog from a prescription diet, check with your vet.

Even on a special diet, it may be possible for you to offer treats or some home-cooked meals, as long as you know what ingredients and nutrients to withhold or limit. And, in some instances, as with the allergic Bichon, preparing your dog's food may be the special diet that is best for managing his health.

Some prescription diets include foods for allergies and food intolerance, for the dissolution or prevention of struvite bladder stones, for treating pancreatitis or gastrointestinal disorders, or to prevent calcium oxalate stones, diabetes, and dental disease. (For more information on these conditions, see Chapter 8.)

Online Help for Prescription Diets

For more information on some prescription diet products, see www.hillspet.com and select the link for "prescription diets," www.purina.com/products/purinaveterinarydiets.asp, or www.iams.com and link to "veterinary products."

Elimination Diets

Special diets may also include elimination diets for Bichons with food-related skin allergies or digestive dysfunction. On an elimination diet, your dog will be restricted to a single, "novel" protein and carbohydrate source.

Novel means that the source is one that your dog should never have eaten before. These proteins can include duck, venison, or fish. Because of the high occurrence of cereal grains as allergens, carbohydrates are usually starchy

Bichons prone to certain health issues may have to be placed on a special diet.

vegetables like potatoes, sweet potatoes, or peas.

While on an elimination diet, treats, edible chew toys, or rawhide-type toys are completely prohibited. The test diet usually lasts anywhere from 4 to 8 weeks, but a trend for improvement or a lack of change may be noticeable within 2 weeks.

Once the trial is ended, a new food may be introduced and can be maintained for as long as no signs of allergies occur.

If allergies return, the elimination diet should be started again; then, your Bichon can either be switched to yet a different food at the end of the trial, or he can be maintained on the hypoallergenic diet.

Bichons on prescription or elimination diets should be closely observed for changes in their health and nutritional status, as well as bladder and bowel habits. If problems occur or if you have questions, contact your vet at once.

SUPPLEMENTS

Dietary supplements can be considered to be any nutrient such as vitamins, minerals, amino acids, cultures, enzymes, and derivatives or complex compounds of these substances. These are the concentrated, isolated versions of ingredients that can be found in various food or organic sources.

In most cases, dogs who are fed a premium-quality complete dry food as the mainstay of their diet are receiving a proper amount of vitamins and minerals in correct ratio. So supplementing with these nutrients is not necessary in most cases.

In fact, some health problems are directly attributable to oversupplementation. Minerals like calcium can contribute to kidney and heart problems, and skeletal malformation. Potassium out of balance with magnesium can result in muscle cramps, heart rhythm irregularities, and digestive upset. Fat soluble vitamins, like vitamin A, can cause liver toxicity in high doses.

If you are feeding a food that requires that you add multiple supplements on a regular basis, this is a strong indication that the food is not meeting your dog's nutritional needs. Look for different ingredients, or another brand—one that provides all the essential nutrients without having to add additional products.

However, some situations may warrant the addition of certain supplements to your dog's diet. Your vet might advise you to provide additional vitamins and minerals if your dog is recovering from surgery, serious illness or an injury, when a temporary increase in these nutrients may facilitate healing. Supplements such as glucosamine and chondroitin may help support joint health in arthritis or patella luxation. Fatty acid supplements may prove beneficial to Bichons with allergies that affect the skin.

Because a nutritious diet is a cornerstone to good health, a proper diet, along with nutritional supplements, may help prevent or relieve symptoms in Bichons prone to various health problems. Before purchasing any supplements and adding them to your dog's diet, consult with your vet about how much and for how long to supplement.

TREATS

The snack of the doggy world, treats are probably available in as many flavours as there are types of dogs. Because treats are not meant as a component of a regular diet, they are not made with nutrition in mind. They are meant to appeal to doggy taste buds—and to an owner's heart when she makes her dog happy by feeding him a treat.

Treats are made using the same variety of ingredients and additives that are used in dry food and semi-moist foods. But they tend to have more flavourings and colour added, and are usually higher in fat, sugars, sodium—and calories! Because of this, a slight reduction should be made in the quantity of main food in your dog's diet to allow for the additional caloric intake if you are going to give

Choosing a Water Source

With white fur that has a penchant for staining around the mouth, it may be preferable to avoid offering your Bichon tap water to drink. Ingredients like chlorine and fluoride in treated water may aggravate a tendency for the fur to discolour. Well water that is high in iron, sulphur, or other minerals that are comprised of naturally occurring chemicals with colour can also result in staining. Additionally, Bichons with allergies must have water that is free of unnecessary components or additives, and those with urinary stones require water that is low in sodium.

People who are conscious of chemical contaminants in tap water may have home water filters installed, or use bottled water for their personal drinking source. Bottled water has usually been specially filtered and "cleaned" before being bottled. Offering this water to your dog is perfectly acceptable.

Other bottled waters available include spring water and distilled water. Distilled water is processed so that all mineral content is removed. It is not intended to be used as drinking water, because it does not contain the nutrients necessary for proper adsorption. Spring water usually is bottled at a natural, ground source and may be filtered to remove any impurities. This water is also a viable option for your Bichon.

Whatever water source you select as best for your dog, make sure that he always has access to a clean bowl filled with fresh water.

Never supplement your Bichon's diet without first checking with his vet

him treats. (And what dog owner is not going to give her Bichon special titbits?)

For the Bichon who is allergic or on a special diet for health conditions such as urinary stones or pancreatitis, treats must be selected with the same extra care as when choosing basic food. Avoid adding any ingredients to which your dog might react or which could exacerbate his problem. It is best to consult with your vet in these circumstances about what types of treats you can offer and how often.

It is possible to buy healthy, lower-calorie, more "natural" treats. Dry treats are preferable over moist ones because they are better for teeth and may contain less artificial additives. Just read labels closely when selecting a healthy treat for your dog. Or, offer him a healthy snack, such as a baby carrot.

If you are eating a healthy meal, it's not unreasonable to give your dog one of your green beans or a nibble of your (lean, low-seasoned) chicken as a treat. Owners who want to go the extra step, or whose dogs are on restricted diets, can prepare treats from scratch. Follow the same guidelines you would as when preparing any healthy meal for your dog, and don't go overboard.

BATTLE OF THE BICHON BULGE

At least once a week, there's a story on the news about obesity: More people are gaining more and more weight. News in the world of pets is the same—more dogs are fatter than ever before.

While not a breed that is highly disposed to storing energy (getting fat!), the Bichon does like to eat and enjoys good food. Bichons do have a slight tendency to overeat a bit, if their food is tasty. And, like people food, so many good-tasting dog foods and treats are available that it's easy for a dog to happily pack on the pounds.

Since a dog can only eat what is put in front of him, it's not his fault if he gets a bit hefty—the responsibility rests squarely on the shoulders of his owner. The best way to treat obesity is to prevent it: Don't overfeed your dog.

This may be easier said than done when those shiny black eyes stare pitifully into yours with a look that says, "I'm going to

Did You Know?

A supplement is a separate nutritional product from your dog's basic food. It is used to add a nutrient that is perceived to be missing from the diet.

faint from hunger; feed me!" Bichons have perfected the ability to wrangle titbits and goodies from their people. When he stands on those hind legs and waves, what are you going to do but respond with food?

The urge to express love and appreciation for your Bichon with food must be resisted. Food is not love. Love means keeping your dog at a healthy weight. Don't give your dog potato crisps or break off some cake for him because you feel guilty. The real guilt comes from allowing your dog to gain weight.

The bottom line is that obesity kills and, at the very least, it reduces the quality of life for your dog. Bichons who are overweight have a greatly increased chance of developing diabetes, heart disease, high blood pressure, digestive disorders, pancreatitis, or liver dysfunction. They can suffer from shortness of breath, decreased stamina and energy, and intolerance to heat.

If your Bichon is overweight, love him back to a healthy weight. The formula for weight loss is pretty simple: Reduce calorie intake, increase caloric burn.

- Cut back on the amount of food each meal.
- Put water on dry food, or add a salt-free, low-calorie rice cake to help your dog feel full.
- Exercise him daily, take him for more or longer walks. If he has health problems that limit his ability to exercise, increase his overall daily activity a little at time, exercising for short periods but more often throughout the day. (Ask your vet about suggesting an exercise plan if your Bichon is overweight and has patella luxation or ACL problems.)
- Offer low-calorie treats like berries, carrots, a lick of fat-free yogurt, melon bites, green beans, or a slice of banana; or buy bite-size, low-cal treats. (If your Bichon has allergies or bladder stones, check with your vet about which fruits or vegetables are safe to substitute for treats.)

Committing to the diet is harder than making the plan. It's nearly impossible to resist those pleading eyes begging you to share a goody with him. But for his health's sake, give him a healthy treat instead and keep him trim.

Did You Know?

Obesity is an increase in body weight caused by the storage of excess fat that exceeds physical requirements.

You'll be surprised what your Bichon will do for a tasty treat!

Can't tell whether or not your Bichon is overweight? Here are some guidelines:

- **Healthy weight.** Ribs can be felt through a minimal layer of fat padding, but are not visible; waist is noticeable when seen from above, has a slight hourglass shape; abdomen appears slightly "tucked up" when seen from the side.

- **Overweight.** Ribs can still be felt but a noticeable layer of excess fat is present; waist still slightly visible when seen from above but may approach width of ribs; abdominal tuck still noticeable, but may approach level of ribs.

- **Obese.** Ribs may be difficult or impossible to feel; fat is thick and visible around lower spine and base of the tail; waist may be impossible to discern; abdominal tuck is gone or may sag below level of ribs.

To be certain your dog's weight is not going too far in the opposite direction, look for the opposite indications: Ribs, spine, and hips are prominently visible; when touched, no padding can be felt; waist is exaggerated, and remaining muscle mass may be drawn into spaces between the ribs and spine; abdomen appears drawn in and tuck is also exaggerated.

If you're still not certain if your dog is overweight or not, ask your vet. She'll tell you if your Bichon needs to lose weight and, if so, how much.

TABLE MANNERS

All dog owners have their own ideas about acceptable behaviour, but you should be consistent when training for table manners.

Begging

Your Bichon doesn't have to beg for his supper, and you shouldn't allow him to beg for yours. If your dog is unoccupied while you eat, he can and probably will pester you to feed him the food off your plate. Don't give in and give him even one little bite. This reinforces the begging and can escalate to the point where he paws, barks, or even steals your food.

To prevent or stop begging behaviour, place your dog in his crate with some fun toys, like a safe chewie. Or put up a baby gate that limits his access to the kitchen while you are cooking and eating. Another option is, after you fill your plates, fill his bowl with dog food and place him in his crate or another room to eat while you are eating.

If you really feel the need to share a bit of your meal, ask your dog to calmly lie down and wait. Then, when you are finished eating, you can give him a bite as a reward for being obedient.

Multiple Dogs

Mealtime etiquette for multiple dogs can be thought of as a formal dinner party, where every guest has an assigned seat. Despite their nature to get along well with other pets, each dog needs his own, separate bowl and eating space. Individual crates or feeding areas in the kitchen and other rooms work well for this. Separation during dinner will keep each dog from having to share his meal and thus prevent any growling, snapping, or hoarding from ever getting started. It's also the only way to make certain that any dogs on a special diet get exactly the food they are supposed to eat.

Give Him Space

Whether your dog eats in his crate or the kitchen, with you

or at his own special time, place his food in his eating area and give him the time to eat. Just as you don't want to be interrupted while you are eating, keep your dog's eating zone free from distractions like playing children, errands that require you to run in and out of the house, or chores that involve noisy appliances.

After your dog finishes his meal, take up his bowl and wash it. If he doesn't finish after a reasonable time (10 to 20 minutes), still pick up his bowl and, if the food contains something that might spoil, like meat, put it away in the refrigerator until the next meal.

If your Bichon pesters you for food while you eat, you must ignore him or the behaviour will never stop.

Picky Eaters

Your dog doesn't have to clean his plate every time he eats, but if his appetite takes a decline, this could be an early sign that health problems are brewing. If your dog is one of those who doesn't like to eat and can be finicky, smell his food. Some picky eaters have a keen sense of smell and, if the odour of the food is not fresh, may refuse to eat. Solution: Change the food to something that smells better or is fresher.

Other reasons may exist why a dog can be finicky or a picky eater. If health and food type aren't the cause, your response is still the same—give him a chance to eat and, if he doesn't, take up his bowl. When he's hungry, he will eat. In few instances will skipping a portion of a single meal upset your dog's health. Only if your vet has advised that missing meals is a problem do you need to worry about getting your Bichon to take his food. Fortunately, most Bichons enjoy their food and being finicky is not a major issue with the breed.

Just as with any other training, sticking to a diet and meal plan and consistently reinforcing proper eating behaviour is good for your dog's health and well-being. You may never take your dog to a public restaurant, but when you have dinner guests or take him out to eat at a friend's house, his table manners will be appreciated.

Food As a Training Tool

Your dog's desire for food can be used as a training tool. Use mealtime as an opportunity to practice basic commands like "sit" and "stay," and offer your Bichon his bowl with huge praise for responding correctly. (For more information on training, including using food, see Chapter 6.)

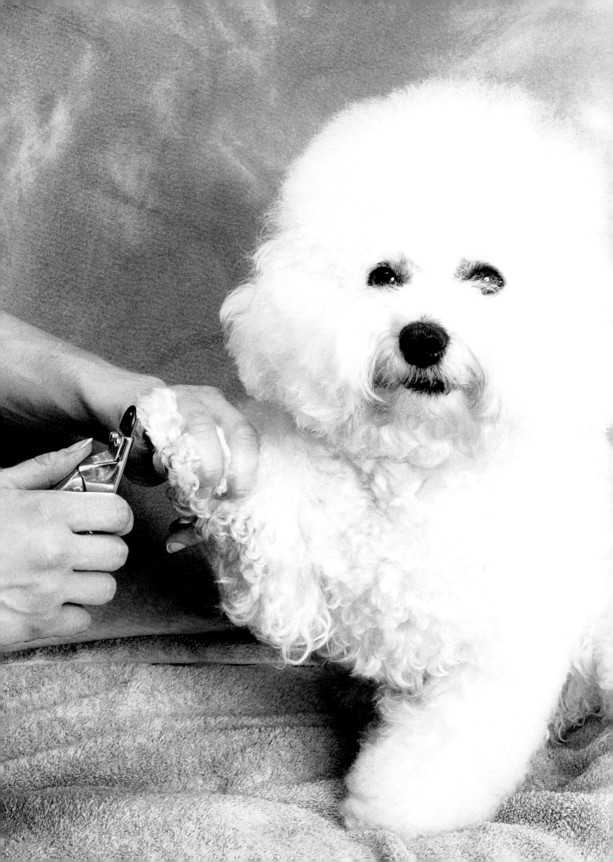

GROOMING

Your Bichon Frise

Behold the beautiful Bichon Frise—a gorgeous cloud of fluffy, white, full-bodied fur. Even the meaning of the Bichon's original French names, *Barbichon* and *Bichon à poil frisé*, refers to their plush coats. *Barbichon* comes from *barbiche*, which refers to a beard or goatee, as does *poil*. *Poil* implies body hair and derives from Latin and Greek words that mean hairiness or a coat of fine, furry hairs. In French, the term *"poil"* is used in phrases to describe tight, curly hair. It is also an expression to say "dandy," the origins of which can be traced to the sixteenth- and seventeenth-century style of tightly curled hair worn by the nobility. Likewise, *frisé* can also refer to curls, but additionally is often used in French to mean crimp, crinkle, or frizzy.

Although *bichonner* is seen today in many French advertisements for hair salons to automobiles, an exact translation is not offered. However, *bichonnée*, the source of the word and breed name, refers to getting dolled up and to being coddled or pampered—something that loving Bichon owners do for their dogs.

PREPARING FOR GROOMING

Unfortunately, the thick curly locks of the Bichon do not beautify themselves into the elegant coat of white cottony fluff for which the breed is known. Part of the pampering that this breed needs is regular and thorough grooming. Commitment to owning a Bichon also means commitment to grooming this high-maintenance breed. Grooming costs can possibly add up each year to nearly half or, in some cases, twice as much as the original purchase price of a puppy. For most owners, maintaining their Bichon's coat consists of a combination of at-home grooming and salon grooming by a professional groomer. Either way, it is wise to be properly prepared for the expense and the time needed for grooming, and to have the proper equipment on hand to get the job done right.

To be successfully groomed, your Bichon must be trained to accept grooming.

Handling

The first step to maintaining that Bichon fluff is training. To be properly groomed, dogs must be trained to accept grooming. The time to start is during puppyhood. Get your dog used to handling by regularly and gently touching his feet, ears, tail, head, eye area, body, and fur. Briefly handle and hold him in a manner similar to what you will do while he is groomed, and reward him with praise and a treat when he behaves and accepts these touches. Let him smell the area where he will stand to be brushed as well as the combs that you'll use on his coat.

With the Bichon, some grooming is more easily done if the dog lies on his side. Start early with training your puppy to lie quietly while you touch him. As he gets used to the tools and the focused touching, gradually increase the amount of time you work with him each session. Add combing to the routine and offer praise when he behaves. Never punish your dog for not being still, because this can teach him to dislike or be fearful of being groomed. Instead, offer treats when he is calm and allows

Don't Forget!

Don't forget to include a doggy toothbrush and toothpaste in your grooming kit.

grooming; this teaches him to look forward to grooming sessions.

For older dogs, such as adopted rescues who may not be used to regular grooming, the same method can be used to help them adapt. An adult dog who may never have received grooming attention may take longer to get used to the routine, particularly if he has had rough handling in the past. But a gentle, positive approach, patience, and treats allows most dogs to learn how to accept being groomed.

Grooming Supplies

Be sure to get the correct equipment for grooming a Bichon.

Combs, Brushes, and Clippers

Purchase the best tools that you can afford. Cheap combs and brushes wear out quickly, and the surfaces of the teeth or bristles can damage fur and result in a greater tendency to mat. Select stainless steel or Teflon-coated combs with widely spaced teeth, in coarse to medium sizes. Small- and fine-toothed combs can be purchased for finishing work, or for combing in the facial area. Combs that offer rotating teeth are available for aiding in mat removal. Some Bichon owners like these combs, while others do not, noting that in some coats the special comb can become tangled in the fur. Slickers are useful for removing debris from the coat and for fluffing. A pin brush, with polished tips, may also be handy for additional brushing after the coat has been combed.

Do-it-yourself groomers also need a set of professional clippers with the proper blades, as well as high-quality, blunt-tipped, curved and straight scissors for trimming and shaping.

Nail Supplies

Along with tools for the coat, buy a good pair of plier-type, small-size nail clippers, and styptic powder. Nail grinders are an easy way to keep doggy toenails trimmed, but may cause problems

Advice From a Groomer

"Dogs have different degrees of accepting grooming" explains Barbara Bird, a Bichon owner and professional groomer. "Some owners may stop if the dog resists or cries, but this reinforces bad behaviour. It's important to teach your dog to positively accept grooming since into every Bichon's life a little detangling and tugging will come. Work on the technique that is least painful to your dog, but at the same time increase your dog's tolerance to any discomfort that might be associated with grooming."

Special Bichon Shampoo Recipe

Here's a home-formula shampoo that owners report works well for Bichons with skin allergies. To make your own, purchase a mild brand of washing up liquid that is advertised as gentle for hands, and mix with additional ingredients as follows:

22 oz (650 ml) mild washing up liquid

2 oz (59 ml) glycerine (available at chemists)

2 cups (.5 l) white vinegar

Put in a gallon (3.8 l) container and fill with water.

for Bichons if the thick curly hair around the toes gets caught around the spinning head. To avoid this problem, push your dog's toenails through a piece of stockings/tights material. This allows the nails to come through while keeping the fur out of the way. Another helpful grooming tool is a small trimmer clipper, designed for trimming hair around the pads of the feet.

Grooming Table

A grooming table with an arm and break-away noose makes the job of maintaining your Bichon much easier. Over-the-table support systems are available that secure the rear of the dog as well, and these help minimise wriggling—especially important during scissor work. Tables provide your dog with a consistent space that he can get used to when you work on him.

Bathing Supplies

Owners who are going to do the full bath at home should purchase additional grooming supplies. A high-velocity dryer that "knocks" the water out of the coat and straightens it as it dries without the use of excess heat is essential.

The choice of shampoo is important for the Bichon, with his sensitive skin. Humans and canines have a significant difference in skin, and pet shampoos come in a wider range of pH than do shampoos for humans. It is all right in some cases to use human shampoo on your Bichon, but be cautious of additives, like fragrances, colouring, and other enhancing ingredients, which could cause skin irritation.

Whitening shampoos for dogs, which are blue or violet and contain deep-cleansing agents, may brighten and correct coat colour. But they may also cause skin irritation in some Bichons. Products for sensitive or dry skin may work best.

For many Bichons, a conditioner helps keep their skin from becoming too dry and their fur from tangling. Avoid products with moisturisers, because they may soften the Bichon coat too much, cause it to fall (lose body), and

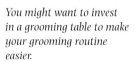

You might want to invest in a grooming table to make your grooming routine easier.

make it spongy or prone to tangling. A dematting spray may also be helpful.

"You don't want to take out the crispness. You want to use a light conditioner," says professional groomer Barbara Bird, "I recommend using a product that contains dimethicone or cyclomethicone. These ingredients have the capacity to cling to and smooth the rough edges of the cuticle, defrizzing the fur without removing body and adding the appearance of reflected light, which will enhance the white without drying the skin."

Comb in small sections, completely from the skin out to the ends.

COAT CARE

Bichons are a double-coated breed, with a fine, silky, shorter undercoat and "guard hairs" that make up the longer, fluffy outer coat.

Combing

To begin grooming a Bichon, place your dog on the grooming table. If you have not purchased a table especially for grooming, you can improvise by placing a nonskid cover or rug on top of a counter, folding table, or washer or dryer.

Combing is necessary to remove dead hair that becomes trapped in the fur and to prevent tangling. Methods, where to start and end, and which combs or brushes to use vary by groomer or owner, but some generally accepted guidelines are suggested. Whatever route you go, work with small sections at a time.

Groomer Barbara Bird likes to work from the bottom up and the back forward, "You always want to be combing over what is already combed because there is less tangling; the comb goes more easily through what has already been done."

Technique in combing or brushing is important. Avoid long strokes that only fluff the outer coat and miss the undercoat, which may cause bunching and matting. Part and lift the fur, comb in small sections, completely from the skin out to the ends. While an overly gentle stroke does not detangle and comb through the Bichon coat as needed, it is also important to avoid rough strokes that may break or damage the coat.

Before or After?

For years, grooming wisdom taught that dogs must be combed before bathing to prevent mats. This was practical advice because wetting tangles often results in a tightening of the mat. But, according to Barbara Bird, this is now considered the "old school" way of grooming a Bichon.

"As a professional groomer, I almost never comb a dry, dirty coat. I only tackle large mats behind the ears, sides of the face, or tail, using a gel that gives maximum slip," Barbara Bird explains. "Mostly I prefer to work on a clean, conditioned coat. Many current products work best after they are dried into the coat. They fill in the hair cuticle, protecting the hair from further damage due to brushing and combing, and allow most tangles to brush right out."

Mat Matters

When you encounter a mat, hold the fur next to the skin to keep it from pulling. First try to separate the mat with your fingers. Next, starting at the bottom of the mat, comb through to the end of the fur. Move higher up in the mat and work the comb down again to the end. This method prevents the tangle from tightening. Repeat until the mat is removed.

Problem areas where mats are more likely to form include inside the back or front legs, the flanks, where the front leg contacts the chest, the cheeks, behind the ears, at the base of the tail, or any location where the dog frequently licks or scratches himself.

For between-bath grooming, Bird suggests misting a light, leave-in conditioner into the area of the coat or tangle where you are working. Don't saturate the fur, only dampen it. Using a spray-in conditioner as you work can eliminate static and prevent tangling. If you prefer not to work with damp fur, try using corn starch instead.

How Often?

In between baths or visits to a groomer, your Bichon must be combed. Recommendations vary on how often to do this, ranging from 10 minutes every day, 15 to 20 minutes two or three times a week, and up to 30 minutes once a week. Judge what is best for your dog's coat type and tolerance for grooming, and plan for these sessions in your schedule.

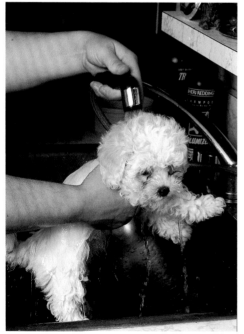

Use a sprayer hose on a tap to bathe your Bichon.

Bathing and Drying

Before bathing, make certain that the coat is tangle- and mat-free. Get your shampoo, conditioner, towels, table, dryer, and tools ready before placing your dog in the water. Chasing a wet, shaking dog around the house makes for a frustrating and messy grooming session.

Bichons are small enough that bathing them in a kitchen sink may be more convenient than in a traditional bath or shower. (Walk-in shower stalls with a seat are easier on your back.) Attach a sprayer hose to the tap if you do not already have one plumbed in for regular use. Adjust the water to a comfortably warm temperature, not so cool it might chill your dog and not so hot that it burns.

How To Bathe Your Bichon

With your dog facing away from the sprayer, and with the stream of water pointing away from his face, lift his head in your hand and gently start wetting him from the top of his head back. Work backwards and down, always keeping the water spraying towards the bottom of the sink or tub so that it is less likely to run into ears or eyes. Some dogs may do better if you place a cotton ball in each ear and some

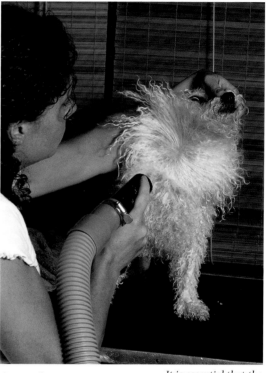

It is essential that the Bichon coat not be allowed to air dry.

petroleum jelly over their eyes before you wet them, thus reducing the amount of water that can enter. Continue wetting your dog's underside by spraying at a downwards angle across his chest and stomach and between his front and back legs. The dog's coat is saturated when a little more water than a drip runs from the fur in all areas.

Shampoo should be mixed with a sufficient quantity of water so that it is slightly thin and runs easily through the coat without having to be worked in, which can cause the fur to tangle. Apply enough shampoo so that it lathers easily, but not so much that it is difficult to rinse out. Start on the back, then the sides. Tip the head up and backward to apply a little shampoo to the top of the head and the neck area. Place some shampoo in your palm to help direct

Grooming As Bonding

Puppies are used to being groomed by their mothers before they even open their eyes. The dam's tongue cleans them and makes them feel secure. As dogs grow, even in the wild, mutual grooming is used as a ritual that unites the pack.

Bichons like routine. This applies to grooming as well. The routine becomes predictable and recognisable. By following an order and schedule, the occasional discomfort that might be associated with grooming becomes acceptable. If you throw in a few treats as a reward, your dog can learn to find grooming enjoyable, and he will love the time you spend with him.

When you groom your dog, he instinctively remembers this nurturing sensation from when he was a baby. Just like dog-to-dog bonding, the time spent grooming your Bichon binds you to each other in a relationship of love, good health, and mutual respect.

it more easily on to the chest, belly, and between the back legs. Be careful around the eyes and underneath the ears. To avoid tangling the fur, lather the shampoo with single-motion strokes, moving in the same direction as the fur. Rinse thoroughly. If you are using a conditioner, apply in the same manner and according to the directions. Again, rinse thoroughly.

How To Dry Your Bichon

The extent of towel drying can be reduced if you teach your dog to "shake off" the excess water first. Shaking is a natural instinct, so when your dog does shake, just praise and reward him while using the phrase "shake" to enforce the behaviour. Then, using medium-thick towels placed fully over the body except for the face, gently squeeze the moisture from the coat without rubbing, once again moving from the head backwards and down. Be sure that the ears are thoroughly dried to prevent water from draining into the ear canal and possibly causing an infection.

It is essential that the Bichon coat not be allowed to air dry. This can cause the coat to droop and turn in on itself as it curls, resulting in a tangled mess. While the coat is still damp, a finishing product may be applied to make final grooming easier. Place your dog on the grooming table (or counter), use the grooming tool best suited for your dog's coat, such as a slicker brush or pin brush, and begin to blow dry on a cool temperature setting while brushing upwards to achieve that stand-out Bichon fluff. The proper technique for combing, bathing, and brushing dry can take about 1 to 2 hours.

Trimming and Scissoring

When it comes to scissoring and shaping the Bichon, several decisions must be made. Do you want a short, easy-to-maintain trim? Or do you want the longer show trim, with all the work that entails? Can you snip and shape your dog well enough to get the Bichon look? Or do you need a professional groomer to mould your dog's coat

into that perfect picture of fluff?

Deciding on coat length may depend on how much time, effort, and money you are willing to put into grooming and maintenance. The main difference between a show trim and a pet trim (sometimes incorrectly referred to as a puppy trim) is simply the length.

Pet Trim

The pet trim is usually between 1/2-inch to 2 inches (1 to 5 cm) long, while the show coat is at least 3 to 4 inches (7 to 10 cm) long. The shorter the trim, the less dirt it can collect, the less likely mats are to form, and the less time it takes to comb, clean, dry, and brush. This style is less sculpted and tends to be the same length over the body and legs, with the head hair cut to fit the length of the rest of the trim.

Show Trim

The show trim is finely sculpted. It is shorter in some areas, such as some parts of the legs, and longer in other areas, such as the head and neck. Show trimming is an art form that takes years

Help—The Groomer Shaved My Bichon!

A frequent complaint owners discuss is how they take their full-coated Bichons to the groomer, and they come back shaved almost to the skin. When the dogs are picked up, owners are horrified and blame the groomer for improper grooming.

While this is sometimes the case, according to Barbara Bird, a very talented and experienced Bichon groomer, more often than not, in these situations, the dog's fur was matted beneath the surface, next to the skin. Bird explains that this usually occurs because the owners, who believe they are doing a good job with maintenance brushing, have been brushing only the top of the coat and missing the undercoat.

To prevent this invisible matting, it is important to detangle the coat all the way to the skin. If you are uncertain how to do this correctly, ask your breeder or groomer to teach you the proper technique. Also, when you take your Bichon to the groomer, ask them to call you if a problem arises, to discuss options before they shave your dog.

Most owners will not have the time to keep up a show trim (left); a shorter pet trim (right) is much easier to care for.

to learn and hours to achieve. If you decide on this style, take your dog to a groomer. Find one who not only has a good reputation for being considerate of the well-being of the animals upon which she works, but also one who has experience with Bichons. Beware of groomers who want to clip your Bichon to resemble a Poodle; this is the sign of a groomer inexperienced with the breed.

Owners can learn to do the show style themselves but, like the professional who has gained her ability through education and experience, it takes plenty of practice to become adept at doing it. If this is your choice, it's still a good idea to start with a professional groomer who will be able to shape the coat into a good foundation from which you are able to work.

Getting a Groomer

Finding a qualified and caring professional to groom your Bichon should be undertaken with the same considerations with which you would choose a kennel or a vet. Important questions to consider include:

- Does the groomer have professional qualifications?
- Does she have sufficient experience in her trade to groom a Bichon properly?
- Is she experienced with dogs, and does she understand their behaviour?
- Are her prices reasonable? Competitive?
- Is the grooming salon clean? Are the grooming implements cleaned between each use?
- Does the groomer competently and happily handle special requests?
- Do the other dogs present appear relaxed or anxious?
- Is the groomer considerate of and patient with the dogs on which she works?
- Does she like dogs and enjoy her work?
- Is she willing to give you a tour or meet your dog and talk to you before you make an initial appointment for grooming?

Study photos of show dogs to learn how to trim and shape your dog. Keep the hair pulled up and out from the body in the coat's ultimate "fluff position" as you scissor. Clip only a little length and small sections at a time. In addition to learning to trim correctly, home-groomers also must learn the proper way to use the scissors.

"You have to learn hand control and how to keep the scissors on a level plane while clipping so that you don't dip too deeply into the fur," explains Barbara Bird. "And you have to learn how to hold and operate the scissors with your thumb only—not a pinching motion with both finger and thumb—so that you make a machine of your hand."

As you scissor your dog, keep in mind that the Bichon cut does not follow the lines of the body. Everything about the Bichon is round and fluffy. The legs are round and do not taper. The body is a series of round curves (but not like Poodle pompoms!). The head is round.

At one time, the head used to be cut so that the ears and beard were longer than the rest of the hair, and the head was rather dome-shaped. This head and facial style evolved into something a little more oval. Today, the current correct cut is round. Although the head has become rounder, the hair on the head is kept slightly longer than elsewhere on the body. Rounding of the fur on the head includes one of the most difficult parts of scissoring the Bichon—correctly shaping the area over the eyes into an "awning" or "ledge." When you have trimmed the head, it should be a perfect circle, somewhat reminiscent of a basketball in shape.

Grooming Frequency

How often you comb, bathe, and trim your Bichon, or take him to the groomers depends on several things. Trim style and fur length also determine grooming frequency, but coat type may be the predominant factor.

Bichon fur can be soft and silky, allowing mats to form quickly; or it can be spongy, slightly "forgiving," and less prone to matting. Some coats can be more or less curly than others. A coarse, kinky coat may also tend to mat quickly.

The age of the dog affects coat type. As noted, the Bichon is a double-coated breed. Puppies only have the soft undercoat, but begin to grow the adult coat between 6 months to 1 year. The adult coat can take many months to fully develop, possibly up to 18 months.

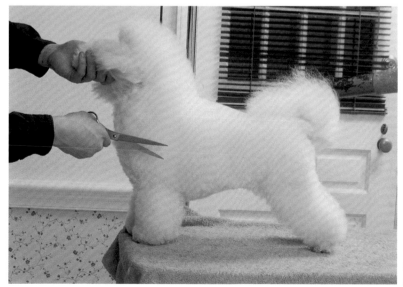

Clip only a little length and small sections at a time.

Puppies seem to mat almost overnight. And the grow-in period can be a trying time as well, while dead hair sheds and gets tangled into the coat. Grooming sessions must be short but frequent during this phase.

Adult Bichons also lose some coat. Even though the breed is considered nonshedding, dead hair does fall out periodically.

Dealing with Doggie Bad Breath

Your dog adores you and jumps into your lap to show you how much. He licks you and breathes on you and—yuck—doggy breath! Not much smells worse than bad breath on a dog. But Bichon breath doesn't have to stink. Some tips for making your Bichon's breath as sweet as his personality are:

- Keep those doggy teeth clean. Brush frequently and have veterinary dental cleanings as often as needed.
- Don't feed food that smells. Premium food with high-grade ingredients is less likely to cause death-breath. And dry food causes less breath odour than canned.
- Toys and treats that offer cleaning and breath-freshening properties are readily available at pet stores.
- Get a vet exam. Many diseases, dental problems, and other health conditions can cause bad breath. Top among these are kidney, liver, or lung disease and malignant melanoma, an aggressive cancer that forms mainly in the mouth.

Correct and regular combing is still required to prevent this hair from collecting in the coat and causing mats.

Some dogs need to be bathed every week or two, while most do well with full grooming every 4 weeks. A few dogs may do all right with regular care every 6 weeks but, by 8 weeks, most Bichons are a mess. Owners must consider each dog's environment and activities, as well as how often they are able to work on maintaining the coat, when determining the best grooming schedule.

DENTAL CARE

Like humans, dogs should brush their teeth after meals, maybe not every meal, but almost as frequently! Small-breed dogs can be more disposed to dental problems, so plan on cleaning your dog's teeth a minimum of once weekly. However, daily brushing is best. Providing safe chew toys that aid in plaque removal and prevent tartar build-up is another way to help keep your dog's teeth clean.

A large variety of doggy toothbrushes, fingertip brushes, and powdered or paste cleaners are available. Never use human toothpaste! Select whichever products keep your dog's teeth the cleanest, are simple to use, and that your dog tolerates best. For the Bichon, a children's toothbrush may be easiest.

It may help your dog to get used to the teeth cleaning ritual more readily if you start by wrapping your finger with a piece of gauze covered with doggy toothpaste. Later, when he accepts your finger in his mouth, move on to a toothbrush. Brush your dog's teeth while he is on the grooming table. Or, if he is calmer, hold him in your lap, supported on one arm like a baby, and use your other hand to clean his teeth.

Although easily overlooked, keeping your Bichon's teeth clean is very important—so keep your dog's pearly whites white and healthy.

Keeping your Bichon's teeth clean is very important.

EAR CARE

The Bichon ear is notorious for its susceptibility to infection, because of the amount of fur that grows under the ear flap, in the exterior of the ear canal. "In some dogs this hair grows so profusely it clogs the passage, keeping wax in and air out," notes groomer Barbara Bird, "If the hair is removed, it prevents problems."

It is standard practice to remove excess ear fur in the Bichon. This can be done by pinching a tiny amount of fur between the fingers and quickly, but gently plucking it out. Hemostats may be used for deeper hairs. Be careful not to pull the hair too aggressively as this can cause redness and swelling at the hair follicles. The overall amount of hair removed depends on how thick the growth is and how tolerant the dog is of the plucking procedure. Cutting the hair with scissors is not an alternative, because the hair is still there to block the passage.

"In most Bichons, the hair in the ears is not deeply embedded," says Bird, "It comes out easily, especially if you use a little powder or cornstarch."

EYE CARE—DEALING WITH TEAR STAINS

White-coated dogs like the Bichon are frequently seen with pinkish, ruddy, or brown stains when their eyes tear. Some reasons for this staining are health related, while others are related to diet and even allergies. This discoloured tearing actually stains the coat.

Hair should be trimmed cautiously away from the rim area of the eye weekly, possibly as often as once a day. Washing this area daily with a cotton ball moistened with warm water or sterile saline helps reduce staining.

Problem Zone

The ear is a problem zone for the Bichon Frise. Don't use an ear cleaner unless your vet recommends it. Cleaners may trigger an infection, or an allergic dog may break out.

Hair should be trimmed cautiously away from the rim area of the eye.

Products specifically formulated for removing tear stains are available from pet stores. Use these products according to directions during routine combing and bathing. Petroleum jelly may be applied directly beneath the eye after thorough cleansing. This prevents the tears from penetrating the fur, thus eliminating the possibility of staining.

Have your dog's eyes examined and treated by your vet if necessary (for more information, see Chapter 8). The most important step in controlling tear stains is to determine and remove the cause.

NAIL TRIMMING

Part of routine grooming for all dogs is trimming toenails. This usually needs done about every 2 weeks. Several types of nail clippers are available for dogs, but many groomers recommend the plier- versus the guillotine-type because they tend to cause less uncomfortable pinching of the nail. A set with a nail guard may be helpful.

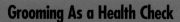

Grooming As a Health Check

Grooming time is the perfect opportunity to give your dog a quick check-up for signs that something may be amiss with his health.

- During combing, does the fur feel and look healthy? Does your dog seem overly sensitive to discomfort?

- In the bath, run your hands over every inch of his body. Are any lumps or bumps present that should not be there? Is the fur or skin too dry or too oily?

- Are the ears clean? Is there an unusual quantity of wax? Does either ear smell badly? Do the eyes have an excessive quantity of tears or is there a mucousy or discoloured discharge?

- Blow-dryers part fur down to the bare skin. Look closely while drying your dog. Are any discolourations present? Is the skin scaly or flaky?

- During nail trimming, check between the pads for debris or burrs that need removing. Check for cuts or abrasions on the pads that may need first aid.

Observe your healthy dog while grooming him. This establishes a baseline against which you can judge what is normal and what is unhealthy in the future.

Before trimming the nails, use small fur clippers or a pair of curved-blade, blunt-tipped scissors to cut away excess hair around the pads and bottom of the feet. When ready to trim toenails, steady the dog with your body and gently but firmly grasp a paw with one hand while operating the clippers with the other. Angle the blades at about 45-degrees away from the bottom of the foot and snip the toenail at the point where it curves, being careful not to pinch or cut into the quick, the tender, sensitive, blood-rich bed around which the nail grows.

If your dog has clearish-white nails, you will be able to see the pink of the quick quite easily, and avoid cutting into it. If your dog has black nails, snip a little at time working slowly back, stopping just before a heavier, white layer of nail shows through the bottom centre of the nail.

Should you accidentally nick the quick, it will bleed and your dog will likely vocalise. Apologise and reassure him that he is fine without making a big fuss, then move on. Stop the bleeding with a styptic pencil or by placing his foot in a container of corn starch.

If you are worried that you might hurt your dog, ask your groomer or a veterinary nurse to show you how to best trim the toenails.

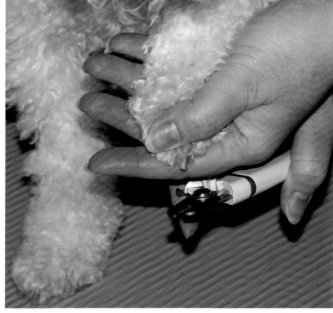

Trim your Bichon's nails about every 2 weeks.

BICHONNÉE YOUR BICHON

Keeping the Bichon looking like a Bichon is a time-consuming and expensive part of the commitment to this breed. Short or long, show or pet style, this dog is a lot of work, but the effort is worth it to those who truly love and care for the breed. In addition to the adorable picture of fluff your dog presents after being groomed, the hours spent grooming deepen the bond between human and dog. Groomer Barbara Bird summarises, "Grooming is a meditation that requires a great deal of patience...and it's a way for the dog to get loving attention from his owner." So get busy and pamper your Bichon with grooming!

6

TRAINING AND BEHAVIOUR
of Your Bichon Frise

How do dogs become good dogs? By training that starts even before you get your dog. Owners first need to research and understand the traits and temperament of the Bichon Frise and study dog behaviour prior to bringing home a Bichon. If you understand dog behaviour in general, it is less likely that your Bichon will become a problem dog in the future. Training is also easier if you understand how dogs think.

Turning a Bichon into a model of canine good citizenship or a well-behaved member of your family should begin the moment you walk through the door. The sooner you begin, the easier it is to shape manners. Teaching a puppy how to live in your home with you is not just a matter of feeding and housetraining. Rather, it is a daily endeavour that establishes ground rules and forms the basis for good behaviour for a lifetime.

Dogs learn new behaviour almost every day, even if it is only how not to get caught when they break the housetraining rules. By ignoring a problem when it arises, you teach your dog bad habits. It's easier to train as you go than to untrain a dog's bad habits. Don't encourage behaviour in a pup that you can't tolerate in an adult dog, or in an adult, behaviour that is acceptable today but may not be tomorrow. In other words, don't allow your Bichon to engage in behaviour that he'll later have to unlearn, then relearn the correct behaviour.

Since dogs don't come already trained and understanding exactly what is expected of them in your home, it's up to you to teach them—with love—just what behaviour is correct and how they should behave. In the early days, when you are forming a relationship with your new Bichon, you will discover that maybe the most important reason to train him is because much of the interaction that bonds you to your dog is training.

TRAINING FOR MANNERS AND MORE

We live with dogs because we love them and they love us. They're cute and funny, and fun to be around...if they are good dogs. Badly behaved dogs are not so much fun as they are frustrating. Even the extra-cute Bichon must be well-mannered so that he is always a pleasure to live with.

Your Bichon must learn to fit into his place in the family structure.

To your dog, your home is his den and your family his pack. Just as in a pack, he must learn the rules for acceptable behaviour. He must also learn to fit into his place in the family structure, with you as the head of the "pack."

Good doggy manners are similar to well-behaved children, acting appropriately in anyone's home or public place. Of course it means housetraining, but it also means good table manners, being polite with company, abiding by house rules, and getting along with others.

Specifically, you must determine what the rules are going to be in your home for your dog. Will he be allowed on the furniture? Do you want to him lie down in a calm stay when guests arrive, until you give the signal that he may greet them? Should he stay out of the rubbish? Is he to remain quiet when he travels in the car? Some owners may not care if their dogs jump up on them or if they bark their heads off when on an outing, but if this is unacceptable behaviour for your Bichon in private or in public, then you must teach him how to act.

Be a Good Leader

Your Bichon looks to you to be the leader—don't disappoint him. Set the rules and stick with them; just be certain that the rules are fair and reasonable. Be consistent in when and how you enforce the rules. Don't let a cute look and wagging tail con you into accepting bad behaviour.

Remember that if you don't take the lead and give your dog directions, he will take over and make up his own rules as he goes along. If he decides to grab a titbit from your plate, and you laugh at how adorable he looks eating your buttered roll in the middle of your bed, not only have you conveyed to him that it's all right to do this, you've also told him he's in charge and he can do and have what he wants, when and where he wants. You've reinforced bad manners and placed his pack status above your own.

As amazing as they are, dogs are not designed to run a household. Your Bichon's security and confidence—and his ability to be well-behaved—all depend on your ability to be a good leader and teacher. Dogs who think they are in charge and are allowed to do what they want are not just problem dogs. They are stressed dogs, and stressed dogs are not happy. Running your "pack" is a lot of pressure to put on such a small animal.

Despite a streak of willfulness and a penchant to persist in obtaining their own way, the Bichon also wants to receive his owner's adoring approval. By telling him exactly what you expect, showing him how to do (or not do) what you want, and then lavishing him with praise when he obeys, your dog will blossom into a well-mannered companion.

Your Bichon looks to you to be the leader of the household.

Hitting Is Not Training

Owners frustrated with a dog who repeatedly does something they do not want him to do may resort to smacking their dog in an attempt to get him to stop the behaviour. Although many decades ago, a rolled newspaper and a whack on the rump may have been considered by some to be an acceptable "training method," it simply is not.

To the inexperienced or old-school owner, the question is "Why?", particularly if a smack has achieved a temporary respite from the unwanted behaviour. The answer is, because hitting is not training, it is punishment. When you hit your dog, you have not taught him correct or acceptable behaviour. You have taught him to fear you and to fear your hands, or whatever item, like a newspaper, you use when you swat him.

To deal with frustrating behaviour, teach correct behaviour. Analyse why your dog is doing what he is doing. Once you understand the reason, find a way to redirect his actions into behaviour that is acceptable to you and him, and that makes sense to your dog.

Dogs do not understand being hit; it has no equivalent in canine behaviour. Instead of hitting, what is it you want your dog to do? When he engages in the behaviour you don't want, stop him with an "eh, eh" sound, then show him what you want. Praise him immediately when he responds correctly. Each time he repeats the undesired action, redirect, then praise. Keep doing this until he gets the idea.

Because dogs may engage in activities that are perfectly

We Are Family

Since your Bichon is part of the family, it is essential that all members of your family understand and abide by the "pack" rules. Although one individual should be responsible for setting these rules, everyone else should agree to them and participate in supporting your dog's learning process.

You can teach your dog how to live the way you want him to be in your home, but do it without hitting.

reasonable to them, but may go against an owner's personal preferences, it is up to the human to provide the dog with a means to understand the diversion of his natural desires. Teach your dog how to live the way you want him to be in your home, but do it without hitting; do it with intelligence, respect, patience, and persistence.

TIME TO GET FORMAL

Probably no better learning experience exists for your dog than a formal training class. It exposes him to a large variety of new dogs, people, sounds, smells, sights, and interesting situations. It stimulates his brain and motivates his curiosity. By providing him with the framework of how to respond to these challenges, you are providing him with a lifetime set of guidelines and coping tools.

Obedience training is not a series of lessons that teaches your dog to do things that you or he will never really use. It is an organised system that trains your dog to be obedient and to respect your leadership.

Another important aspect of formal training is owner education. In doggy class, you will learn to understand how your dog thinks. You'll learn how to set clear training goals for your dog and have him understand what you want. The classes teach you how to teach him—how to effectively interact and communicate with him.

When you get home, you and he will have a ready-made means for working on home manners and proper behaviour. Everything you teach from here, whether it's to be a good companion, basic obedience, or advanced training for competition or therapy work, will be built on the solid foundation you have laid.

Like dogs, dog training comes in many forms, from individual instructors teaching small groups, to private trainers working with a single dog per lesson, to obedience training clubs that have several instructors on staff directing various sizes and levels of classes. Research your options to decide what will work best for you and your Bichon.

How To Find a Trainer

A good place to start searching for the right trainer is to ask your dog-owning friends and neighbours with well-behaved dogs where they went for training. Were they happy with the instructor and the instruction methods? If not, why?

Ask your groomer and vet for referrals. Look on notice boards in pet stores or veterinary clinics for flyers and business cards posted by training clubs and private instructors. Check to see if your veterinary clinic or even your local rehoming centre offer training as part of their services. Watch for advertisements in the newspaper. Look in the phonebook under "Pet," or "Dog Training." Find out if a local community centre schedules obedience classes. You can also query a search engine on the Internet for training resources in your area.

Once you have found a training group, ask the instructor questions:

- Professional trainers do not have to be certified, but is the trainer you're considering approved by any organisation or board? If so, what requirements did they have to meet to become certified? How does their certification relate to their experience in training dogs?
- How much and what type of experience does the trainer have?
- How many years have they taught professionally?
- Is the instructor knowledgeable about dogs and do they understand dog behaviour? Are they educated about different training methods and techniques?
- Has the trainer ever worked with Bichons? Are they willing to assist you and your dog with your specific concerns?
- Are they willing to use the best training methods for your Bichon and not just a single style they have always used? If the instructor uses force-into-position techniques and punishment-style corrections, it is probably not the best class for a Bichon.

Schedule a time to observe an instructor's class. If he is unwilling for you to watch, take this as warning sign that something is amiss and find another option.

Types of Training

Another major criteria for selecting a training instructor is the methods she uses and whether those methods will work for your Bichon. With so many types of training methods, the average owner can become confused trying to understand how each works when making a choice.

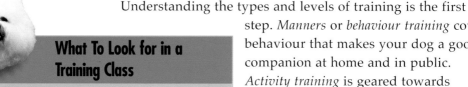

What To Look for in a Training Class

You should observe a training class before you enroll your Bichon. While there, watch for the following:

- Is there a goal and plan for the class?
- Are the instructions focused and understandable?
- Does the trainer like the dogs and people with whom she is working?
- Are the methods positive, and are correct actions rewarded with praise?
- Are the dogs nervous and uncertain, or are they happy and relaxed?
- Are the people and dogs learning?
- Are the fees reasonable or worth the value?
- Bottom line, is this an instructor and environment where you and your dog can train and learn?

Understanding the types and levels of training is the first step. *Manners* or *behaviour training* covers behaviour that makes your dog a good companion at home and in public. *Activity training* is geared towards teaching your dog how to perform or compete in specific events or work, such as flyball, agility, dance, therapy, service, and so forth. *Basic obedience* is usually a prerequisite before attending training classes for a specific activity.

Obedience training is the beginning of more formal commands such as Sit and Stay. It serves many purposes, including facilitating manners training, and offers varying degrees of difficulty, but the focus is on what the dog does, and how quickly and how well he responds to commands. Classes teach standard commands that have been around for decades (more information follows in this chapter).

Over the years, many techniques have been developed to teach and enforce these commands. Training methods can be divided into two categories: compulsive, where the dog is forced to learn behaviour; and inducive, where the dog is persuaded to learn the behaviour.

Older, less in-favour methods use force and punishment, and can include heavy-handed correction, compulsion, discipline, stern tones, and harsh handling. These methods are currently out of favour except for the most difficult or aggressive dogs. Considered inhumane by some instructors, they are definitely not the way to go to train a soft-tempered Bichon.

Lure Training

Lure training is a method in which an object that a dog likes, such as a favourite toy or treat, is used to coax him into the desired behaviour. The dog is taught to watch and follow the object, is told what to do, then rewarded and praised when the desired position is given in response. As training progresses, the lure is phased out and praise becomes the reward. The initial lure can then be given after the training session.

A variation on lure training is play training. The theory behind this method is that, before a dog will work for his person, the two must be able to play together. The dog learns to relax and play in settings other than his home. Then training moves on to the standard commands, using a toy as the lure.

Natural Training

Natural training focuses on the emotions and behaviours that drive a dog. It is a technique that believes the use of treats, toys, compulsion, or punishment are all wrong. "Proper" training is based on understanding and working with a dog's innate nature and learning how to communicate with him in a way that a dog really understands, to get him to do what you want. Praise and correction are given by touch, body language, and voice. The development of a cooperative relationship is a central key to this type of training.

Lure training uses an object your dog likes, like a toy, to coax him into the desired behaviour.

Positive Motivation

Positive motivation is reward-based training that uses no compulsion or punishment. Corrections are only done in a positive, teaching manner so that the dog knows what you want. Incorrect behaviour is ignored, and the dog is redirected toward the correct behaviour with no reaction. When the dog responds correctly, he is rewarded with treats. To signal correct behaviour, the dog is often given a "jackpot" of treats, communicating to him in an obvious manner when he has responded well. Owners are taught to build a "history" of positive reinforcement with their Bichon outside of training by rewarding him lavishly for good behaviour. Bad behaviour is thwarted by prevention. For example, if you don't want your shoes chewed, don't leave them where your dog can get them. In class, dogs are trained in flat collars only, using standard leads and plenty of praise, petting, toys, food, and play. The use of lures or clickers is often employed.

What Is a Reinforcer?

In training, a reinforcer is an item or action that reinforces a particular behaviour. Positive reinforcement could mean the use of praise or treats. It is also possible to have negative reinforcers, but the use of negative reinforcements such as an ear pinch (Ouch!!), to prevent unwanted behaviour are no longer recommended.

Clicker Training

Clicker training is a more involved form of training that was originally used to teach large marine animals performance tricks. In recent years, it has been applied to dog training and the now very popular technique has had quite a bit of success.

Traditional training uses praise as both a reward and a motivational reinforcer for correct responses. Clicker training breaks this single step into two components so that the click signal clarifies for the dog which exact behaviour it was that earned him a reward, thus allowing him to understand more precisely what behaviour is expected from him when a command is given.

If your dog is across the room and correctly responds to your command, a click—which he will learn to associate with rewards—can be given to tell him he did well, since you can't give him a treat from a distance. Clickers can also be used with dogs who get so excited by treat rewards that they can't work, or for those few Bichons who are not food motivated. The click will still be identified as a positive response.

Clickers work as a "secondary reinforcer." A "primary reinforcer" is the rewards—food, a toy, or being petted—for which

No matter what type of instruction you choose for your Bichon, make the commitment and stick with it—for your Bichon's sake.

your dog is motivated to work. A secondary reinforcer becomes associated in your dog's mind with these rewards. An example of primary and secondary reinforcers is when you pick up your car keys and jangle them in your dog's direction. In excited anticipation of a trip in the car, he runs for the door. In this case, the primary reinforcer is the trip, but the keys—the secondary reinforcer—are associated with the car outing that he enjoys.

Clicker training is a more involved method and, if you want to give it a try with your dog, it's wise to register for a training class in which the instructor teaches you the proper use of the clicker. The advantages of clicker training are many: immediate feedback, clear identification of proper behaviours, association of the training work with rewards, and positive motivation—a necessity with a Bichon.

Whatever type of instruction you choose as best for your

Bichon, make a commitment to be faithful to the endeavour and to your dog, whose behaviour and emotional well-being largely depend on the foundation of good training. Whether it's household manners or formal training, remember that a dog is constantly learning. Talk to him. Without rambling on, simply explain to him what you expect or want him to do. By doing so, you will learn to understand your dog and your dog will learn to listen to you and look to you for guidance on correct behaviour. Teach him well, and teach him throughout his lifetime.

CRATE TRAINING

As soon as your new Bichon comes through your door, you should have his own space ready and waiting for him. Just like a kid having her own bedroom, a crate is a bedroom for your dog. Crates are not doggy jails. They are a safe, secure personal haven where your dog can eat, retreat, rest, recover, and even play.

When you are making plans to bring home your new dog, put selecting an appropriate crate at the top of the list. (More information on selecting and preparing a crate can be found in Chapter 3.)

Location

Place your Bichon's crate in a location that is dry, warm, and free from drafts in the winter, and pleasant in the summer months. It should be in a room, such as your bedroom, where you spend much of your time. Your dog should be able to see, or at least hear and smell you from his crate. In the early days, particularly with a young puppy, it is best to set up the crate near your bed. Other possible locations are the kitchen or a family room, places that are central to family activities, conveniently close to the feeding area, or to an exit to the garden, but not busy with traffic from people entering or leaving the house.

Teaching Your Bichon To Like the Crate

Once you have set up the crate and got it ready, teach your dog that this is his special place. Show him that it is his space alone, a space he can enjoy. Entice him to enter the crate initially by putting some treats in the back. At first, allow him to wander in, smell around, and wander back out. Don't shove him in and shut the door. A few safe toys will make the crate a place where he wants to

A crate is a safe, secure personal haven for your Bichon.

stay. Feeding him his meals in the crate will also make your Bichon realise his crate is a good place to be.

How long it takes your Bichon to get used to his crate depends on his personality. Some dogs take to their crates immediately, others may need a few days to get used to the idea, and a few may resist, pawing at the door and barking to get out every time you shut the door.

In actuality, very few dogs are truly claustrophobic; most are just insistent on getting their way when they want to be near you or engaged in another activity. It is important that you continue to work with a Bichon like this to teach him to accept his crate, because crate-training is a cornerstone of good behaviour. Don't give in to your Bichon's efforts to convince you that putting him in his crate is a terrible torture that he cannot tolerate. Gently tap your finger against the front-top of the crate and tell him, "Quiet." When he settles down, even if only a bit, you can let him out. Then, to continue training him to the crate, place him back in the crate again with a few treats.

As your dog calms down and goes into his crate on his own, praise him. In the early days, while you are gently manoeuvring your dog into his crate, use a phrase like, "get in your crate" or "go to bed," so that he begins to associate your request with being crated—and liking it. Gradually increase the amount of time your dog spends in his crate.

How Long Can He Stay in the Crate?

Crates are not a substitute for taking care of and watching

over your dog. Puppies need to be taken out to their toileting area about every 2 hours, and adult dogs should not be crated more than 4 hours at a time without a break. The exception to this rule is when your Bichon is put in his crate overnight.

In addition to serving as your dog's den, a crate keeps him safe and out of trouble when you can't watch him, gives him a space to get away from activity when the household is busy, and keeps him from escaping or getting stepped on when company visits. The crate is not only a miniature home for your Bichon, it is an excellent training tool and should become one of your dog's favourite places to be.

HOUSETRAINING

You will be amazed at how frequently small puppies need to relieve themselves. They are generally eating 4 meals a day, and have access to fresh drinking water—and the results are inevitable.

One of the most important items on a dog owner's teaching list is reliable housetraining. Although it is also likely the most tedious and time-consuming training job you ever undertake, it is crucial that you don't shortcut the process or overlook failures. To do so practically ensures a lifetime of puddles on your carpet.

Choosing a Spot

Before you bring your puppy home, have an outdoor area picked out to use as his "toilet area." This spot should be conveniently reached from an easily accessed door in all types weather. Sometimes it helps your dog understand that this is time for business if you use a door separate from the one he uses to go out for play, car trips, and walks. Ideally, the area will be located close to where you can efficiently dispose of faeces when it's time for clean-up duty.

Getting Started

The first time you come home with your new dog, take him directly to this spot and allow him to smell it thoroughly. Give him enough of a chance to go, but don't stay so long he doesn't know why he's there. Encourage him with a verbal command, such as "busy." If he does, praise him, acting as if it's the most exciting act in the world (but don't yell so enthusiastically you scare him!). If

How Long Is Too Long?

You cannot ask your Bichon to stay in his crate for long periods of time. Puppies need a potty break about every 2 hours, and adult dogs should not be crated more than 4 hours at a time without a break. Even with outdoor breaks, your dog should not be crated longer than a total of 8 to 9 hours a day, except during the night beside your bed when he is young.

Have an outdoor area dedicated for your Bichon's toilet use.

Those Subtle Signs

How do you know if your puppy needs to go? Sometimes it's not easy to tell, but watch for a rapid shift in attention, sniffing, circling, frantic activity, running back and forth, or a quick awkward movement as if he's not sure if he wants to sit or not.

he doesn't toilet after a while, go inside and crate him.

Immediately upon letting your dog out of his crate, take him out to his toilet area. Don't just send him outside and hope he goes—you have to make certain. It is absolutely essential that you praise, praise, praise him when he toilets. Go ahead— sound silly, let your neighbours think you are crazy. Your puppy must know from your praise that his toileting outdoors makes you ecstatic. With most Bichons, a little treat reward may help reinforce the behaviour.

Supervision Is Key

While you are waiting on your pup to toilet, don't play with him or allow him to wander around. He must understand the difference between play time and toileting time. Again, if he doesn't go, return him to his crate and try again soon. To stay out of the crate, your Bichon puppy must earn the privilege by relieving himself outside.

Once he has toileted, he can remain outside his crate for exercise and cuddling. However, you must not let him out of your sight. Watch him every single second for any sign that he's getting ready to empty his bladder. Puppies can realise quite suddenly that they need to urinate. They often don't give much noticeable warning, but a subtle sign may occur. Watch for a rapid shift in attention, sniffing, circling, frantic activity, running back and forth, a quick awkward movement as if he's not sure if he wants to sit or not. At any of these signals, rush him to his toilet spot and instruct him to be "busy".

Fortunately, the signs that your puppy is about to evacuate his bowels are a little more noticeable, and occur on a more regular basis, usually within about 15 to 60 minutes after eating. He will need to urinate about every 2 hours, and after he eats, after he has a treat, after playing, after sleeping, in the morning when he wakes up, and at night before he goes to bed.

Even though it may be time to return your dog to his crate, if he has just toileted, give him a few more minutes of freedom so that he learns to associate being out of his crate with toileting outdoors. Confinement is a key element to your Bichon's understanding of where it is all right to relieve himself and where it is not.

As your puppy gets the idea that every room is also like a den and must be kept free of his waste, you can gradually expand the area in which he is allowed while out of his crate, but still under your supervision. Do not allow him into more space than you can watch until he becomes reliably housetrained.

One way to ensure constant supervision is the "umbilical" method. Clip your Bichon's collar to a long lead that is tethered to your belt, belt loop, waist, or wrist. Your dog will be close but somewhat on his own while you are likewise somewhat free to engage in other activities. When he moves, you will be better able to notice any signals that indicate he is about to relieve himself, and you can react by promptly taking him out.

Accidents Happen

Despite your vigilance, your puppy will have an accident in the house. If you are watching him, as you should be while he is out of his crate, you can catch him in the act. Interrupt him by startling him with a phrase like, "not inside" or "outside," and immediately scoop him up even if he is still in the middle of relieving himself. Rush him out to his toilet spot, place him where he can finish the job he started and urge him to be "busy" outside.

At the accident site, do not, under any circumstances, ever, hit your dog, rub his nose in the mess, or scold him. When he comes back in, return him to his crate and clean the spot thoroughly. It is important that your dog understands that it is not his relieving himself that is the problem, rather the location.

Place the papers or rag with which you first soak up the urine in his outdoor toilet area so that he understands that this is where he is supposed to go. Smelling his urine there and hearing you tell him "good spot" will help reinforce the idea that emptying his bladder outside is good and the behaviour you want. With his keen canine nose, it is possible that your Bichon may detect some remaining odour of urine in the spot you have cleaned. And, like outside, that odour may make him want to urinate there again. Some dogs can be deflected from this by telling them "bad spot" and moving them from the area to another activity. Clean the spot again, and keep on housetraining.

The Crate As a Housetraining Tool

As a housetraining tool, crates excel at teaching your puppy bladder and bowel control. Dogs are born with a natural instinct to keep their dens clean. While your puppy is confined in his crate, he will avoid eliminating in order not to soil his area or himself. Although he will not relieve himself while confined, puppies have limited control and storage capacity and must be taken out frequently.

Puppies have small bladders, so you'll have to take them out regularly.

Cleaning Up Puddles

To prevent your Bichon from urinating on a previously used spot on your carpet, completely remove the urine and its odour from the fibres, and possibly from the underlay as well.

- Suction up urine with a handheld wet-vac, or blot it thoroughly with newspapers and paper towels weighted down on to the urine-soaked area. If using paper to blot, you may need to change the paper several times.
- After removing as much urine as possible, apply an enzyme cleaner specifically manufactured for dog urine. The product should break down the protein in the urine and remove the odour. Follow the manufacturer's instructions, then blot up any excess product.
- Spots can be washed with cool water and a pet-specific carpet cleaning chemical if needed. Follow product instructions, and remove excess liquid.
- Let the carpet dry before allowing your dog on the spot. If he still sniffs the area with interest, repeat the procedure.
- In some instances, urine may soak through to the underlay. Carpeting may need to be peeled back to reach the underlay for cleaning. Although less likely with a dog the size of a Bichon, it is possible, for carpeting that is repeatedly soaked, for urine to penetrate through the underlay and into the subfloor. In such cases, it will probably be necessary to remove the old carpet and underlay, replace the affected subfloor boards, and reinstall new flooring.

It is much easier to clean urine from hard-surface flooring than it is from carpeting. However, it is important to remove it quickly to prevent seepage into the joints, such as the grout in tile, as well as to prevent your Bichon from smelling urine in an inappropriate location.

- Wipe up urine with paper towels or rags. Wash rags thoroughly.
- Use a cleaner specifically indicated for the floor type, but that is also safe for pets.

• Rinse with a damp cloth or moistened paper towels and dry.

Housetraining an Adult

When adopting an adult dog, such as from a rehoming centre or rescue group, it is possible he may not be completely housetrained, or he may have forgotten his housetraining due to improper care. With these special-needs dogs, go back to step one and start from the very beginning, exactly as you would with a puppy. Although most adult dogs are able to hold their urine longer than a puppy, there may be co-existing health problems that necessitate going out just as often.

Remember too that small dogs in general and the Bichon in particular can present a greater challenge to housetrain to total dependability. Regardless of age, weather, or other intervening conditions, faithful adherence to housetraining procedures is mandatory if your Bichon is going to become—and remain—the clean, well-behaved, indoor companion he is meant to be.

You've Lost That Denning Instinct

What happens when a puppy is placed in a kennel or exercise pen and ignored when he needs to relieve himself? What about a rescue dog who may have spent most of his life in a small cage or contained in one room? Any normally clean dog can lose his natural instinct to keep his den clean under such circumstances.

Despite his best efforts to keep from soiling his own space, eventually any dog will have to go where he spends his time. And eventually, out of necessity, he will overcome his distaste for soiling.

These Bichons can be retrained, but it will present a greater challenge that requires more time and effort than usual. Personal space in a crate must be as small as possible while still maintaining comfort. The dog must be taken out more often and, at the least little indication he might have to go. When he does toilet, effusive praise should be given along with jackpot-type food rewards to impress upon him the positive importance of changing his habits.

If he relieves himself in his crate, promptly remove him, take him out, along with any bedding containing the scent of the urine or faeces, and proceed as with usual housetraining. Do not show any displeasure with your dog. If any of the waste gets

Special Circumstances

On occasion, bad weather, illness, or other events may interrupt his routine. For example, some Bichons do not like to go to toilet in the snow. Try shovelling an area down to the grass to provide access to his usual toilet area. For owners who live in flats, Bichons can even be taught to use a litterbox if this is the only option. Newspaper can be placed in a garage for other special circumstances. Teach your dog to use these areas just as you would if he is to go outside.

on his fur, wash it off. Clean his crate thoroughly and give him a chance to play. Praise him for being clean. Stay diligent about normal housetraining routines until he regains his preference for a clean den. Even old Bichons can learn new toilet tricks.

LEAD TRAINING

Put a lead on some puppies and as soon as they feel a little tug on their necks, they'll lay down and start "screaming." Fortunately this is seldom the case with a Bichon, but if you have a "screamer," you'll need to teach him how to walk on lead.

Start with getting your puppy used to a collar—a nylon one with a break-away buckle usually works best. Select a size that is slightly larger than your puppy's neck and adjust it so that you can easily slip three to four fingers beneath it. Make certain to adjust it as your puppy grows. A few dogs will scratch or attempt to bite at a collar when you first put it on them, but most quickly forget its presence as soon as feeding or play time begins.

For walking a Bichon, choose a lead that is long enough to easily reach his level without you having to stretch or pull on his neck. The material should be durable but not heavy, and the lead should be comfortable for you to hold in your hand.

Start indoors: Let your puppy smell the lead, then clip it to his collar. One method is to let your puppy drag the lead around on the floor while you supervise. As he adapts to its presence, you pick it up and, using a treat, entice him to come to you.

Another technique is to show the puppy that through the lead you are connected to each other. When he walks around you follow him. This will get his attention. As he watches you walking with him, show him a treat and walk away from him, still holding the lead and enticing him to now follow you and the treat you

Bichon Toilet Troubles

Why are Bichons more difficult to housetrain than some other breeds?

- Because they're adorable. It's hard to make a bundle of fluff go out in the rain if he doesn't want to go.

- Because they give you that cute look. When they make a mistake, it's more difficult to enforce proper behaviour because they talk you out of sticking to the rules.

- Because they're small. It's easier to hide your indoor toilet area if you're Bichon-size and harder for a much larger human to find all those not-so-accessible spots when they're behind the couch or under the bed.

- Because it takes more time and consistent effort than any other training.

- Because the Bichon is prone to urinary tract stones and bladder infections. These conditions can cause a more urgent and frequent need to urinate. Other health problems that can affect housetraining may include diabetes, heart disease, kidney disease, certain medications, special diets, hypothyroidism, Cushing syndrome, inflammatory bowel disease, pancreatitis, parasite infestation, and more. Check with your vet if your Bichon has any change in bowel or bladder habits.

- Additional inappropriate urination or defaecation can be caused by separation anxiety, submissive urination, intense play, upon greeting visitors (this occurs more frequently in young dogs), or marking of territory by dominant, unneutered, or unspayed dogs.

are holding. Praise and offer treats as he continues to follow you around. Eventually, take him outside and repeat the procedure. Soon he will learn that his lead is associated with pleasant activities like outings.

Bichons who have tracheal problems, or have had neck, back, or spinal injuries may be more comfortable walking on lead wearing a harness instead of a collar.

BASIC OBEDIENCE

Bichons are a "soft" dog, with feelings and a spirit that can easily be broken. They are also reputed to be stubborn and hard to train. In reality, they have distinct personalities that must be accommodated.

Analyse the situation if your Bichon is resistant to learning basic commands and work out how to get his attention. As one-time circus entertainers, it is in the Bichon's nature to learn and repeat an action, like "waving," that earns him applause. Walking beside you in heel may not make sense to your dog, so you must give him a logical reason—rewards and praise—for doing it correctly.

"Positive training works brilliantly for the Bichon. They work well for toys and food," says Natalie Bayless, a Bichon owner and professional trainer. "Positive training does take more work because you have to do the exercises more often and maintain more variety. You have to use more reinforcement with more creativity. Be generous with praise and rewards and be patient."

Whether you are about to embark on a formal training adventure or just work on basic obedience commands at home, these guidelines can prove useful for teaching your Bichon. In addition to verbal commands, you may want to begin your training by using hand signals along with the word. This way, your dog receives both a vocal and visual clue as to which requested behaviour you want him to perform. Ask your instructor to show you the simplest hand signals for training your Bichon.

It's a Scream

There's no other way to describe it—some Bichons will emit a doggy-type "scream" if you try and force them to do something they don't want to do. To non-dog people it probably sounds like you're trying to hurt your dog!

Praise and treats can get your Bichon to walk nicely on his lead.

Training Time

The Bichon seems to learn better if training sessions are not so long as to become boring or repetitive. Length of home practice sessions should vary based on each individual dog's attention span and the purpose of your training.

Most formal dog obedience classes last about 60 to 90 minutes, and instructors recommend that owners practice at home at least two or three times a week between classes. Watch your dog for signs of loss of attention after about 15 or 30 minutes—wandering gaze, wandering off, sloppy performance—and be ready to end on a positive note, with a command successfully completed.

If you are training your Bichon for formal competition, then you and your dog should probably practice more frequently and for slightly longer sessions. However, it is still possible to break even lengthier training sessions into shorter episodes; instead of 1 hour once during a day, try two half-hour sessions.

Sit

To teach your dog to sit, seat yourself on the floor and have treats at the ready. Hold a treat just above his head and slowly move it backwards. As his eyes follow the treat, he will usually sit. If he walks backward instead, guide him by using your other hand to gently slide down his rear and place him into a sitting position.

When he sits say, "Good boy, good sit" with great enthusiasm and give him the treat. Practice this until he understands that "sit" equals a reward, and he can respond without you on the floor or with a treat over his head. As training progresses, your Bichon will learn to sit beside you when you come to a stop during a walk.

Down

This command can be started from the Sit command, since your dog will already be halfway in position. A dominant Bichon may not like being in a down posture, because it can be interpreted as a signal of submission, but with enough encouragement and positive reinforcement, he will learn it is an acceptable and praised response. He will also eventually learn to go into a Down from a standing position.

With your dog in the Sit position, take the treat and slowly lower it to the ground in front of your dog. Without pushing, lay your other hand, if necessary, on his mid-back to indicate that he should not rise or stand. As he starts to crouch into a Down, move the treat so that he must slide into a full lying position to reach it. You may need to bend over beside or kneel next to your dog to accomplish this. When he is down, say "Good boy, good down" and give him the treat. Do not ask him to remain in the Down position very long while he is first learning the command. As he gets used to the position, training will progress to where you are standing up while he lies down.

Stay

Stay is nearly always paired with the Sit or Down commands. Earlier in his training, your dog may be more accepting of learning the command from a Sit position, especially if he does not enjoy Down.

Begin with your dog on your left side. In a firm voice that goes down in pitch (think of the sound of a motor winding down to a standstill), say the word "Stay." At the same time, move your open hand, palm towards dog, out from your left leg about 45 degrees. Step out with your right foot—a signal to indicate that he should remain while you leave. Take a couple steps, then turn, and stand in front of your dog. After a few seconds, return to your dog's side and praise him, "Good stay, good boy."

If your dog gets up, get his attention with a sound like "eh, eh" ("no" or "bad" are far too strong) and guide him back into position. When first training, you can repeat the command and hand signal until he understands what you want, then gradually eliminate this practice as he learns. Standing with your left foot on his lead (without applying any pressure to his collar) may also help him comprehend that he is to remain in his spot, without using a coercive correction.

Gradually increase your distance and the time he is in Stay as you practice the command. Stay should be taught in small increments at a time, only moving to greater times and distances when your dog responds correctly to your smaller requests.

The treats used in training should be small, soft titbits than can be eaten quickly.

Come

To have your dog come to you when called is the best command he can learn, and it's a command that may possibly save his life should he ever get away from you. The key to success is to make your dog want to come to you all the time. Never call him to come, then punish him or do something to him he doesn't like, such as plucking his ears. By doing this, he will learn to associate coming with discomfort and will probably run in the opposite direction. Instead, always offer praise when he comes to you.

Begin teaching Come with your dog on lead. Reel the lead out until it is loose, then reverse your direction, without turning around but by walking quickly backwards. As you walk, tell him to "come, come, come" in a high-pitched, happy, and excited voice. When he comes toward you, gather the lead so he won't run past. Praise him, "Good come," and give him a favourite treat...or two.

As he gets used to "come," add the "sit" command to your routine, having him sit in front of you. Avoid calling your dog, particularly early in training, when you are unable to enforce the command. A good way to reinforce this command and associate

Training Treats

One trick to successfully using treats as a reward is to offer small, softer titbits that can be eaten quickly. Hard, crunchy, or larger treats—like bone-shaped biscuits or baby carrots—take too long to chew. Possibilities include semi-moist treats, niblets of cheese, or dried, cooked liver. If your Bichon is on a restricted diet, check with your vet about which treats are safe for him.

it with positive things is to use it when you call him for dinner, "Bichon buddy, come and get your supper."

Heel

This command will save your dog's neck and your wrist, and make your daily walks less of a fight and more of a delight. To teach your dog to heel, have him sit on your left side. Step off with your left foot, a signal to indicate you are going to walk and he should come with you. Say, "heel" and start walking.

Since most Bichons are easily lead-trained, he should get up and get moving with you, but if he lags behind, coax him along with a treat in your hand held at the level where you want him to walk. If he tugs or rushes in front, don't let him drag you along. Gently reel him back in, repeat the command, and slip the lead behind your waist so that it is impossible for him to forge ahead.

As you walk with him by your side in proper position, tell him "good heel." With practice, you will be able to reduce your repetition of the verbal command and to unwrap the lead back to its normal position, hanging at your side.

Stand

Start teaching the Stand command with your dog in a Sit-Stay. Turn to face his side. With your right hand, hold a treat close to his nose, and while saying "stand," move the treat slightly up and away from his face. As he gets up and begins to lean towards the treat, but before he can take a step, slide your left hand under his belly towards his back legs and say, "Good stand, good boy." Your arm is just a guide to the correct position, not a way to force him into it. Eventually, you will teach your Bichon to stand and stay.

Training Tips

Once you've taught your dog the basic obedience commands, you can use his ability to learn and your skills to train to teach him tricks he will enjoy performing, and which will amuse your family and friends. Your Bichon will love the attention and applause he gets for his performance.

- Whatever command or trick you teach, remember to break it down into small increments, and always, always praise your dog when he responds correctly. Set specific and clear training goals and know how you are going to achieve them.

Down, Stay, and Stand—Why Are They Useful?

- "Down" can be useful when you want your dog to lie quietly (and more comfortably than a prolonged Sit) while you are busy with another task. Down may be practical to use during some veterinary procedures.

- In competition, the goal of Stay training is to leave the dog unattended in the Stay for a set period. In real life, it is to get your dog to hold a position as long as needed, for example, when he is being groomed or receiving medical treatment.

- The Stand command is useful during veterinary exams or while your Bichon is being groomed.

- Involve the whole family, both in class and at home when practicing. Show each one in your household which commands you are teaching your dog and which methods you are using. Be consistent in your approach and be patient. Learning takes time.

- Communicate concisely what it is you want your dog to do. Remember that commands are statements, not questions. Select specific words or phrases to use when praising, correcting, or training. Do not mix commands. For example, saying, "come on and sit down," will only prevent him from understanding what you want him to do. And use the correct command for each situation. Telling your Bichon "down" when you really mean "off" will confuse him so that he does not know which response you want.

Establishing eye contact is very important when training your Bichon.

- Never yell or hit, and don't train when you are frustrated or angry with your Bichon. Be firm but loving. Whether it's training for competition or fun, the working relationship that comes from training, along with lots of praise, will provide you and your dog the opportunity to spend quality time together.

SOCIALISATION

Dogs are social animals; it's in their genetic make up. Without social exposure they wither; with social contact they thrive. Even as companionable as the Bichon is, your dog needs socialisation to be the sociable butterfly he was born to be.

Without socialisation, your dog will not know how to properly act around people or other dogs. He could also become fearful, timid, or overly protective.

Socialisation is a word that's thrown around quite a bit by those in the know in the dog world, but what does it really mean? Summary of dictionary definitions means "to prepare for cooperative living."

Roughly translated into doggy-speak, socialisation means to expose your dog in a controlled and positive manner to a wide variety of people, animals, places, sounds, smells, and objects and to teach him how to respond correctly to these differing situations.

It should start when he is a puppy and continue through his lifetime.

You socialise your dog through an infinite variety of situations, and each requires the proper approach. In general, explain in short, but precise words to your dog what you are doing (or where you are going) and what you expect from him. This may help him learn to associate certain terms with specific situations—and outcomes—which he can then learn to expect. Be calm as you introduce your dog to the new place or person. Act as if what you are doing is normal and occurs all the time. If your dog gets hyper, tell him to "settle." If he is fearful, avoid reacting to him in a manner that reinforces this behaviour. Don't force him to investigate, but don't withdraw abruptly. Start slowly and build gradually. Try little excursions, like taking your Bichon with you to the local shops. Or, have a neighbour meet you at a park to walk your dog.

Dogs who are well-socialised are happy, well-balanced, and well-behaved, with the ability to adapt to new situations. Socialisation helps prevent behaviour issues from developing. Bichons are a perfect breed with which to socialise. By being with you when you are out socially, your dog will quickly learn to enjoy being a polite canine socialite.

Other Useful Commands

- **Drop it.** Teaches your dog to drop an item already in his mouth when you cannot reach him.

- **Enough.** Indicates that the activity in which your dog is engaging is not bad, but it has limits, such as inappropriate timing or duration. When it's time for him to stop doing something, "enough" tells him to stop.

- **Give.** Teaches your dog to hand you either an object that he already has but shouldn't or a toy that you want him to give up.

- **Leave it.** Teaches your dog not to pick up items that you don't want him to have. This command can prevent him from chewing or eating dangerous objects, spoiled food on the ground, dropped laundry.

- **Off or out.** Handy for getting your dog off or out of places where he doesn't belong or that might be unsafe for him.

- **Wait.** Teaches your dog to wait at the door, or before getting out of the car, while you get his lead, etc.. This command can prevent bolting behaviour, and it teaches patience.

If you're uncertain how to teach your Bichon these additional commands, ask your trainer for assistance.

PROBLEM BEHAVIOURS

Canine behaviour can be a puzzle to an uninformed person. Sometimes it's funny or cute, other times it's disastrous—at least as far as humans are concerned. Before you get upset with your Bichon, understand that what may be unacceptable to you is not to your dog. Learn how to determine if his behaviour is normal and needs modification so he can live in harmony with you, or if the behaviour is abnormal and requires the intervention of a professional.

Aggression (Dog–Dog)

Bichons tend to be very friendly with other dogs, animals, and people. However, it is always smart to keep an eye on your dog when he's around other animals. It's safer for him. And, if he shows any tendencies to be aggressive, the behaviour can be stopped. Study dog-to-dog communication so that you understand the difference between normal behaviour and aggression. It's normal for dogs to communicate with each other about status and territory, so this communication should be permitted. However, if your dog is being aggressive towards another dog, tell him "no" and put him in his crate. Be cautious how you break up dogs who are fighting so that you do not accidentally get injured or bitten.

Biting, Snapping, and Nipping

Most puppies use their mouths and will nip during play. From dog to dog, this is normal, but it is behaviour that must be discouraged from dog to human. A dog should learn that it is never acceptable to put his teeth on a human. When your puppy nips you, startle him with a loud "Ouch!" and move away. This mirrors the behaviour of his littermates, and acts as a signal to him to stop rough play. Substituting a toy may also redirect his desire to nip. If your dog continues to nip as a part of play, add a firm "no bite" command and stop playing with him. Your Bichon will soon get the message that nipping is not fun.

A well-socialised Bichon gets along with other dogs and with different types of people.

Snapping or biting is different from nipping. It has nothing to do with play and everything to do with dominance, aggression, or both. A Bichon who uses snapping and biting to communicate his displeasure is a dog who thinks he's in charge. Snapping is usually a preliminary step to biting, and it must be addressed immediately. The best method of dealing with biting is prevention. This is done by training that clearly indicates to your dog that you are the alpha. In most situations, help from a professional is desirable.

Dogs bite for many reasons—protection of property, fear, as a reaction to sudden pain, as an indicator of territory, and as a message of displeasure. In most cases, these reasons can be

"Normal" Behaviour

- Mouthing or chewing; "talking" or vocalising during play; some barking.

- Cautious but curious; investigates by removing objects from cupboards and rubbish.

- Active, energetic; easily distracted, short attention span while playing, especially puppies.

- Avoids direct eye contact until after you have lived and trained together for a while.

- Plays by pawing, batting at, or pouncing on toys, other pets, or people.

- Rolls over on back.

- Wants to be with you, follows you, or wants to lay against you.

- Rolls in animal droppings.

described as a warning for the perceived offender to stop and as an attempt to protect himself or his owner. Whatever the reason, biting is *never* acceptable.

Listen again. Biting is *never* acceptable. (The only possible exception to this rule is if the dog is defending you from an attacker or is actually defending himself from physical abuse. Keep in mind however, that the dog who learns to bite due to abuse is a seriously troubled dog.)

What You Can Do

If your dog shows warning signs, such as growling or snapping at you before biting, tell him very sternly, "No bite." Remove any toy, treat, or activity that could be considered by your dog as a reward and put him into a Sit-Stay. If he bites, or if his behaviour continues to deteriorate into biting, get help. Have him checked by a vet for a hidden illness or injury, particularly if your Bichon has never shown any inclination towards biting behaviour before.

The sad part about a dog who bites is that it's not his fault. Somewhere, somehow a human is to blame. A tendency to bite may be genetic, a bad disposition inherited from a relative; dogs with a bad temperament should never be bred from. If caught early enough during puppyhood, it may be possible to eliminate this behaviour, but it will take an educated, dedicated, and ever-vigilant owner to prevent biting from developing into a serious problem.

In rescues, a history of abuse, sometimes even of punitive-type training, can cause an otherwise good-tempered dog to begin biting. These dogs may also be trained to stop this undesirable behaviour, but not always. Again, owners must put in extensive special effort to reverse the behaviour.

Occasionally, if a puppy's nipping is ignored, and if the behaviour is reinforced by the owner laughing at, accepting, or otherwise encouraging the dog, nipping can develop into snapping and biting. Dominance biting is a difficult behaviour to reverse.

Dogs who bite are dangerous. They are a liability, and they are bad news for good dogs everywhere. Because of their small size, some owners may not take it seriously when their Bichon bites. A bite from a Bichon is not cute. A dog who bites is a stressed, miserable dog. Because the conclusion to an episode of biting is often tragic, don't ignore the warning signs or the behaviour. Early intervention is critical if the dog is to be saved. If your Bichon bites, seek professional help.

Chewing

Bichons are no bigger chewers than any other breed but, like any other dog, they do mouth and they do enjoy a good chew. The solutions to destructive chewing are simple: prevention, supervision, and redirection.

Watch your puppy while he is playing. If you are supervising his play time, he won't have the opportunity to chew on furniture or any other off-limits items. For large items that can't be removed, place a bit of hot sauce, or vinegar on the area where your dog likes to chew.

To a puppy, if it's on the floor or within reach, it's fair game for chewing. Keep shoes, remotes, pencils, children's toys, or anything else that you don't want chewed, put up or shut away from your pup's reach.

Dogs and puppies need to chew, especially when they are teething. Keep your Bichon supplied with plenty of safe, chew toys. Should your dog get hold of a non-chew item, use the "give" command and take it away. Immediately substitute a chew toy, then tell him "good boy" when he takes it.

Digging

Digging is not necessarily a favourite past time of the Bichon. Dogs dig for a variety of reasons: something to do, when pursuing small prey such as rabbits or moles, to make a spot in which to lay, to get out of a fenced garden.

The most frequent reason for digging is because it's fun. If your Bichon is a digger, consider providing him with a sandbox, which can be used for digging. Fill the box with white, filtered sand (cleaner for that hard-to-groom white fur of his), and toys. Once you show him that digging is acceptable here and that the box and toys are his, this usually curbs his tendency to dig elsewhere.

What Does "Alpha" Mean?

Alpha is the first letter in the Greek alphabet. When the term is applied to dogs, it means the leader of the pack — or the "first" dog. Dogs like structure, so it is important to them that each member of a pack has a rank, such as alpha, or leader. Ranking within a pack determines which dog eats first, gets the first choice of the best bed or toys, and so forth. By having a pack hierarchy, the chances of fighting are greatly reduced since every member knows his place and rights.

Even if your Bichon is the only dog in the house, pack rank is still important to him. In his eyes, you are a member of the pack. And, as the responsible human of this group, it is up to you to be the alpha — a dog should never be allowed to run a household, no matter how clever he is!

"Abnormal" Behaviour

- Biting, snapping, or attempting to bite; growling or aggression towards people or other pets; makes and maintains eye contact in an intimidating manner; possessive of food, toys, or bed.

- Overly shy, timid, or fearful; wants to hide most of the time; frequent cowering or cringing.

- Hyperactivity, inability to concentrate or focus attention even briefly.

- Continuous or repetitious barking or crying.

If your dog is making a comfy spot for himself, try placing an outdoor bed for him on a patio or deck. If he's trying to escape, secure the bottom of the fence line. For any type of digging, when you catch him in the act, tell him, "No dig," redirect his activity by showing him a toy, and then praise him.

"He's Too Small To Be Dangerous"

Because of their small size, some owners may not take it seriously when their Bichon bites. But a bite from any dog—even a little Bichon—is not cute. A dog who bites is a stressed, miserable dog. Don't ignore this behaviour—seek professional help.

Excessive Barking

Just like humans, dogs talk, some more than others. Usually it's because they have information they wish to communicate to us. A novel idea in dog training is to listen to what your dog has to tell you, then thank him for the message. If he continues to bark, tell him "enough."

If neighbours are complaining about your dog barking while you aren't home, it may be a symptom of *separation anxiety*. This type of barking is handled differently (see more information in the section on Separation Anxiety).

At other times, your dog must be quiet, such as when you are on the phone. Tell him "no bark" and place a finger over your lips, whispering "sshhh." This should get his attention and, when he responds, tell him "good quiet, good sshhh." "Quiet" can actually be taught when your dog is not barking—while he is being quiet, just tell him, "Good quiet." Try tying this into clicker training so that he understands the exact quiet behaviour for which he is being rewarded.

Houdini Syndrome

Despite their preference for human company, owners note that their Bichons are little escape artists. Crates and fences are no match for these clever dogs, who often work out how to unfasten lift-type latches. Outdoors, they are small enough to get under fences that aren't secured against the ground.

If your Bichon is engaged in destructive chewing, redirect him to chew on something appropriate.

To keep your dog from getting away outside, determine why he wants to get out. Many reasons may exist, each with its own solution. While you are working at resolving the problem, secure the garden and prevent his escape. Indoors, pick a safe crate with a pinch-type latch that requires opposable thumbs to open. Your Bichon may be smart, but he can't work these kinds of fasteners.

Jumping Up

This is a tough one for every dog person. When you really love your dog, you probably also love it when he eagerly greets you, jumping up for a kiss and hug. But times may occur when this is not practical—if you're wearing fragile clothing, carrying packages, or if you don't feel well. And what about when visitors come to your house? Some people don't want any dog to jump on them at any time. (Hard to believe, but true.)

Keep your Bichon secure— these little escape artists can learn to unfasten lift-type latches.

Greeting a pack leader who's returning to the den is normal behaviour in dogs. They gather around to smell him and lick his muzzle, signaling the togetherness of the pack. When you return home, this is what your dog is doing. Jumping is your dog's adaptation to be able to reach the taller members of his pack.

You must decide if your Bichon is going to be allowed to greet you by jumping. If you don't want him to jump up, it is necessary to teach him not to do this, then consistently stick to the rules. Being allowed to jump sometimes but not others can be quite confusing for your dog. How is he supposed to know the difference between when it's all right to jump and when it's not?

Teaching "No Jump"

To teach your Bichon not to jump, you should have taught him some basic obedience commands, particularly "sit," "stay," "wait," and "off." Go out the door, then come back in. When your dog jumps on you say, "off, no jump." Firmly but carefully push him back down and turn away from him. Tell him "sit" and "stay." Praise him for obeying, then stoop to his level and allow him to greet you as exuberantly as he wishes from the Sit position. Release him from his Sit and continue your entry as you normally would when you return.

Eventually switch the Sit-Stay to "wait" once he has learned not to jump. Using "wait," your dog can continue standing or walking about while he awaits your greeting, and you don't

To Jump or Not To Jump?

It's up to you to decide if you'll allow your Bichon to greet you by jumping up. If you decide it's not okay, you must be consistent. Expecting your Bichon to understand that jumping on you in certain situations (e.g., when you come home from the gym) and not others (e.g., when you're wearing your best clothes) is not fair, and will only lead to confusion.

An open litter bin can be irresistible to your thieving Bichon.

have to remember to release him from a Stay. The important message is that your Bichon still gets to greet you without jumping up on you.

Laundry Thieves and Other Thievery

Bichon owners have many stories about their breed's propensity to steal. They seem to have a peculiar, unique preference for taking men's socks and women's lingerie and eating them. The simple answer to this "problem" behaviour is to promptly deposit dirty underwear in the laundry basket.

Owners report that Bichons like to take and hide pens, toilet paper rolls, Kleenex, and other small items. They also like to get into the litter bin and take out discarded rubbish. These problems are preventable by placing all small items out of your dog's reach. Rubbish can be kept safe by placing it in a container with a lid that fastens, or in a sack inside a cabinet with a childproof hook.

Separation Anxiety

Owners want their Bichons to bond with them; they are an affectionate dog, bred to be companions. But can your dog be too dependent? The answer is Yes. Separation anxiety is probably the number-one behaviour issue in the Bichon.

Other than the obvious—that your dog becomes anxious when you are separated from him—what does it mean to be overly dependent? An overly dependent dog has a higher than normal need to always be near his human.

Only a thin line exists between bonding and dependence. Bonded means a close, healthy relationship that is enjoyable for both dog and owner, one in which the human can be away from her dog without negative repercussions. But the dependent dog becomes extremely agitated when he is not in the company of his owner. Bichons who suffer from separation anxiety are not just unhappy when their owner isn't around, they are profoundly distressed.

Behaviours that indicate a dog may have separation anxiety include panting, whining, pacing, drooling, occasionally vomiting, and inappropriate urination or defaecation when the owner is away. Bichons with this problem tend to bark or howl nonstop until their owners return. Related behaviours that can develop are depression, loss of appetite, self-induced injury like lick granulomas, excessive barking, howling, and destructive conduct such as shredding clothing, digging up flooring, and chewing or scratching doors.

The possible reasons for separation anxiety are poorly understood. Lack of socialisation, genetics and poor breeding, a history of neglect, or puppies who have been taken from their mother too soon are all theories as to the cause.

Owners might even play a part by being excessively needy themselves, or emotionally dramatic around or overly protective of their dog. A dog who always gets his way, or demands and receives too much attention, may be more likely to become too dependent. As a dog bred to be a close companion, the Bichon may have a greater than usual need to be near his person, and he may react more noticeably to any of these triggers with separation anxiety.

Prevention

The best way to deal with emotional dependence is to prevent it. Reduce the possibility of your Bichon becoming too dependent on just one person by having different family members feed him. Ask a friend or neighbour to take him for a walk or car trip. When it's necessary to separate your dog from yourself, instead of closing a door, put up a baby gate through which he can still see you.

Provide structure and routine in his daily life, while at the same time exposing him to interesting new situations. Make sure your dog has his own space, where he feels happy and secure. And remember training—a formal, classroom setting where your dog receives positive basic instruction is one of the best means of providing the exposure and confidence that helps prevent separation anxiety.

Overdependence

Separation anxiety may be the number-one behaviour problem in Bichons. As a dog bred to be a close companion, the Bichon may have a greater than usual need to be near his person, and he can react to emotional upheaval and overdependence with separation anxiety.

Desensitization

If your Bichon already shows signs of separation anxiety, work on desensitising him to your departures. Practice placing your dog in his crate with a safe toy, then go outside for a few minutes. When you come back inside, leave him in his crate for a moment. Repeat this procedure, gradually extending the amount of time you are out.

Don't make a fuss about departures and returns, because they are

Is Your Bichon Dependent?

Traits that may show a tendency towards dependency:

- Timidity or shyness

- Fearful, startles easily

- Inability to adapt to change

- Overly protective of family, home, vehicle, or possessions

- Destructive when not occupied with owner; lack of interest in playing by himself

- Easily stressed, mildly hyper-reactive, both emotionally and physically

- Rescued dog; background of suspected abuse and neglect

a normal part of household routine that your dog needs to accept. Try changing your departure ritual by removing the clues you are leaving—leave your keys in the garage, put your coat in the car, park on the street instead of in the drive.

You can also act as if you're leaving, then don't. Put on your jacket, pick up your keys, walk toward the door, then turn around, and sit down instead. Shortly, get up and put away your keys and jacket without leaving. Repetition of this scenario allows your dog to become less sensitive to departure cues.

When you leave, keep a radio playing and a light on, place an item of clothing that smells like you in his crate and allow access to toys that will keep your Bichon happily occupied until you return home to him. Although it doesn't work in all situations, a canine companion for your Bichon may also reduce his anxiety while you are away.

BEHAVIOUR SPECIALISTS

Sometimes, a dog will develop a problem that basic training cannot help. Dogs are complex characters, and it's possible that even the best, most educated and responsible of owners won't have the right answer on how to resolve their dog's issues. When you are in over your head with bad or baffling behaviour, it may be time to consult an animal behaviourist.

Behaviour specialists are educated to understand dogs, their body language, communication methods, pack structure, and much more. Most behaviourists come from a background in psychology and are certified through the International Association of Pet Behaviour Counsellors (APBC). If you want an appointment with a behaviourist, you will first need to get a letter from your vet. The behaviourist will work with you to establish the cause of your Bichon's behaviour and develop treatment and training plans that are suitable to your circumstances. The APBC also runs seminars and workshops if you want to gain a fuller understanding of canine behaviour. For more information visit the APBC website (www.apbc.org.uk).

Some professional trainers may be competent at providing you with behavioural consultations. Be cautious using this approach— are they really qualified to help your dog with his problem? Additionally, some behaviourists with psychology degrees may limit their practice to animals but lack animal behaviour

A behaviour specialist can be an excellent resource for any problem you feel you cannot handle alone.

certification. They may be able to help, but make certain that they understand dog psychology and are capable of translating this understanding into a plan that resolves your dog's issue.

What To Look for in a Specialist

Ask about their credentials, references, and history of professional experience. If your dog requires medication as part of his treatment plan, find out if the behaviour specialist has access to a veterinary specialist with whom they can work? When selecting a behaviourist, ask if they have experience with Toy dogs.

"A Bichon is a Toy dog by biology," says Darlene Arden, author, lecturer, and certified dog behaviour consultant specialising in issues of dogs 20 pounds (9 kg) and smaller, "This means the Bichon has special considerations and will respond like a Toy dog. They need positive behaviour modification methods."

How do you know if your dog needs a behaviourist? Any sudden or extreme change in behaviour, or behaviour that has been deteriorating for a while might be an indication. Start with a thorough veterinary exam first. About 20 percent of abnormal dog behaviours are a result of a medical problem. (Some veterinary specialists estimate the incidence even higher, up to a third.)

Whatever the cause, don't be afraid to get help from a behaviour specialist. It could be the difference that turns your Bichon into the happy dog he was meant to be.

7

ADVANCED TRAINING AND ACTIVITIES

With Your Bichon Frise

art of the pleasure of having a dog is spending time with him. Some of that time will be spent just being together under the same roof, with both of you engaged in different activities. But if you want to get more out of your time and relationship, more active pastimes exist in which the two of you can engage.

You can enter numerous regulated competitions, and there are leisure activities that just help you unwind or get healthy. Whatever activities you choose for you and your dog, the two of you will be working as a team, learning something new, maybe helping other people, and definitely enhancing the bond you and your Bichon share.

DOG SPORT SAFETY

Before engaging in any competition or strenuous activity, your dog should be thoroughly examined and cleared by a vet. For the Bichon, this means paying particular attention to little legs that are prone to problems. Vaccinations should be up to date (or antibody titers sufficiently high) so that your dog is protected against disease. In addition:

- Slip-proof your dog. Trim the hair short around his feet and foot pads, cut his toenails. If the surface where he will be competing is slippery (mats are usually used) apply a "sticky paw" product.
- Use the right collar for the type of activity. The wrong collar or dangling ID tags may interfere with your dog's performance or cause an accident. A properly sized collar and lead is also important to correct performance.
- Some sports include obstacles. When dogs are first learning above-ground obstacles, use a second person as a spotter to reduce the chance of falls.
- If your dog is injured, sick, or showing early signs of any change in health,

don't compete. At competitions, avoid getting too close to any other dogs who look or act as if they are ill. If your bitch is in season, you may not be permitted at some events. At those where she is allowed, keep her crated away from intact males! Teach your dog "no sniff" in regards to greeting other dogs and enforce the no-smell zone.

- Come prepared. Bring your dog's home away from home (his crate and bed). Pack plenty of clean bowls, bottled water, dry food, and treats. Make sure you bring all the supplies you need to compete, like brushes, balls, and so forth, plus extra leads, proper ID, first aid kit, and copies of medical records or group credentials if needed. A folding chair for down time is handy, as are extra plastic bags for poop patrol.
- Dress for the weather; leave an umbrella in your car or tack box. During hot weather, bring ice packs, extra water, and tarpaulins or pop-up shelters for creating shade, maybe fans and extension leads if there is electric supply. For cold temperatures, bring a doggy sweater and booties if it's icy or extremely cold. Pack an extra blanket and towels. Keep a watchful eye on your dog if the weather is extreme.
- Always watch your dog. Keep him safe from bigger dogs, fast-moving people feet and out of show supplies that can cause injury. Let him relax, but don't let him misbehave.

AGILITY

Probably the most popular competitive dog sport going, agility, is high-action excitement and fun for owner and dog. Trials are run on a course of obstacles through which the handler must successfully direct her dog in a limited amount of time.

Obstacles include jumps, tunnels, tyres, see-saws, weave poles, elevated walks, A-frames, and more. Because agility is like play, most dogs, Bichons included, enjoy the work. The fast pace and audience enthusiasm create an atmosphere that is well-suited for the Bichon as entertainer.

A folding chair can come in handy during down times at outdoor events.

Even though it's a "fun" sport, dogs who compete in agility should have a solid foundation in obedience training and work well with their owners. "I put my Bichons through a basic obedience course prior to trying agility work," says Nancy Bayless, a Bichon owner and professional trainer whose Bichon Rufus has earned Masters level titles in two different agility organisations.

Because some Bichons are prone to knee problems, agility may not be the best sport for them. But even a shorter-legged or slower Bichon can enjoy agility. Agility events in the UK are run under Kennel Club rules, and dogs are not allowed to compete until they are 18 months of age. This is a safeguard to protect bones and joints, which are vulnerable while a dog is still growing. Bichons, along with other small dogs, compete over small-size hurdles, and the tyre will also be lowered. The contact equipment is the same for all sizes of dog.

When your Bichon is ready to start competing, it will start at elementary level, and progress its way up the classes, with each stage becoming increasingly challenging for handler and dog.

Good To Know

Most agility classes only accept dogs who have successfully completed a formal obedience class.

What Makes an Agility Dog?

What does it take to make an agility dog? "I got Jillian when she was about 8 months old. Her previous owners couldn't deal with a dog who was airborne all the time," says owner Fran Davis of her Mach-2 Bichon, "I knew immediately she had the makings of an agility champion."

A natural aptitude is just the start. Fran says she built a bond of trust with her dog first. Then she took Jillian along to agility classes to watch while she trained her other dog. Jillian got so excited she seemed to be asking to try the sport too. Like Nancy Bayless, Fran started her Bichon in basic obedience.

Training, even for a fun sport like agility, must be enjoyable if a Bichon is going to succeed. "The Bichon thrives on variety, so try not to practice the same sequence repetitively," Nancy explains.

Possible problem areas for the Bichon include a Down-Stay on the low pause table, which may be perceived as threatening for the small dog. A-frames are mountainous and may likewise take some extra work. But Nancy believes that most Bichons, particularly the more thinly built dogs, are good jumpers and need very little instruction to get going. Fran says that her dog loves to jump and do the obstacles and,

Dress for Success — Agility

Dress should be tailored casual, and loose fitting for running. Some participants wear tailored knits that stretch for movement, but return to a tighter fit when standing. Some competitions have handlers wearing matching outfits. Khakis and golf shirts are popular. Quality athletic shoes are important.

Agility consists of obstacles like jumps, A-frames, and tunnels.

once she became involved with the sport, Jillian just "took off."

Another bonus when training the Bichon for agility is his natural inclination to gaze at his human's face. Because he has a high desire to please, a Bichon looks into his owner's eyes for cues on what to do next, a huge plus when running an agility course. This trait can be used in training for other competitive sports as well.

Clues work both ways; keep an eye on your Bichon to make sure he is having fun competing. "If a Bichon gets overly stressed from competition, they will leave the ring to visit spectators," Nancy says, "If they're having a good time, they'll blitz around the course."

Bichons and their people can have tremendous fun competing to earn some of the agility titles that are on offer. Fran gives a little advice for those thinking about trying agility with their Bichon: The focus should not be on winning, but on having a sense of accomplishment and fun.

GOOD CITIZENS

For a dog such as the Bichon who frequently goes out in public or travels with his owner, being trained and well-mannered is essential. Earning a Good Citizen Dog Scheme title is a way to offer proof of good behaviour, particularly to non-dog persons and to businesses or motels that might be reluctant to admit a dog.

The Good Citizen Dog Scheme is a training programme that was designed by the Kennel Club.

Since its launch in 1992 in excess of 52,000 dogs in the United Kingdom have passed the test, which is administered by more than 4,000 training organisations nationwide.

The Good Citizen Dog Scheme is aimed at all dogs, pedigrees and non-pedigrees, regardless of whether they are registered with the Kennel Club. There is no age limit for dogs taking part.

There are three levels of award to aim for. These are bronze, silver and gold, with each level becoming increasingly more difficult.

The Awards: Bronze Award

Dog and handler must complete the following exercises:

1. Cleanliness and identification: The handler carries some form of 'poop-scoop'. The dog wears a collar and ID tag.
2. Collar and lead: The handler puts on a correctly fitting collar and lead.
3. Walk on lead: The dog walks on a loose lead, without distractions.
4. Control at door/gate: The handler walks through a gate with the dog under control.
5. Controlled walk among people and dogs: The dog walks on a loose lead, ignoring distractions, and sitting quietly while the handler holds a conversation for one minute.
6. Stay on lead for one minute: With the dog in the sit, stand or down.

A well-trained Bichon can be trusted to behave in many different situations.

To prepare for the Good Citizen Scheme, your Bichon should have received basic obedience training.

7. Groom: The dog accepts all over grooming without protest.
8. Present for examination: The examiner observes the handler who conducts a full examination of the dog, including mouth, teeth, throat, eyes, ears and feet.
9. Return to handler: The dog is released from the lead, and is then recalled by the handler.
10. Responsibility and care: Questions are asked to test the handler's knowledge relating to dog care and ownership.

Silver Award

Dog and handler must complete the following exercises:

1. Play with the dog: A short, controlled game to show interaction between dog and handler.
2. Road walk: Testing the dog's ability to walk on-lead under control.
3. Rejoin the handler: The dog remains steady when the handler leaves, and rejoins on command.
4. Stay in one place: The dog must stay in position for two minutes, with the handler remaining in sight.
5. Vehicle control: The handler gets the dog in and out of a car in a controlled manner.
6. Come away from distractions: The handler remains in control, despite distractions of people/dogs.
7. Controlled greeting: The dog greets a person without jumping up.

8. Food manners: The dog must not beg or snatch when people are eating.
9. Examination of the dog: The dog allows inspection of its body by a stranger (as might be undertaken by a vet).
10. Responsibility and care: Questions are asked to test the handler's knowledge relating to dog care and ownership.

Gold Award

Dog and handler must complete the following exercises:

1. Road walk: Dog and handler walk along a road, turn, stop at a kerb, and cross a road. The dog must be under control, and changes of pace should be shown.
2. Return to handler's side: When the dog is off-lead (not less than 10 paces away), the dog is recalled and returns to the walking handler's side. The pair should continue together for approximately 10 paces.
3. Walk free beside handler: The dog walks at the handler's side, off-lead for approximately 40 paces, including two changes of direction.
4. Stay down in one place: The dog remains in position for two minutes while the handler moves out of sight and returns.
5. Send the dog to bed: The dog is sent to its bed (blanket or mat) on command.
6. Stop the dog: To stop the dog at a distance in an emergency situation. The dog is off lead, and the handler is at a distance of 20 paces.
7. Relaxed isolation: The dog is fastened to a 2 metre line, and must remain calm and quiet for two to five minutes while the handler is out of sight.
8. Food manners: The dog is offered food by hand or in a bowl, and waits for permission to eat.

9. Examination of the dog: The dog allows inspection by a stranger (as might be undertaken by a vet). This includes mouth, teeth, throat, eyes, ears and feet.
10. Responsibility and care: Questions are asked to test the handler's knowledge relating to dog care and ownership.

FLYBALL

Flyball is a team sport for dogs that was invented in California in the 1970s. It now has an enthusiastic international following. This active sport is perfect for Bichons who love to

If your Bichon loves to run and catch balls, flyball might be right for him.

run fast or catch balls. Flyball is a relay race played by one team of dogs against another. Four dogs per team each take a turn racing and jumping over four hurdles to a box, where they must step on a spring that releases a ball. The dog must catch the ball, then jump back over the hurdles on his return to the starting line. As soon as he gets back, another dog takes off, until all dogs have run.

Teams compete in elimination heats until one team of dogs comes out a winner. The height of the hurdles is based on the height of the shortest dog on the team. Minimum jump height is 8 inches. Hurdles are spaced evenly apart over a distance of about 50 feet (15 m).

In addition to teams winning a flyball tournament, individual dogs earn titles based on a point system.

Is Flyball Right for Your Bichon?

How can you tell if your Bichon might like flyball? According to Lynn Speedie, who regularly competes with her Flyball Master Bichon Poppy, the best indicators are that they are "ball crazy," love to play fetch, and enjoy tug games. Training used to take about 6 months, but with current methods using classroom practice, manuals, and videos, training from start to tournament can take as little as 12 weeks.

If you know your Bichon loves to run and play with balls, encourage him to learn to catch the ball. This may be the first step, but other traits make up a flyball dog. "A dog can be taught to fetch a ball, but a good flyball dog really has a lot of drive to run *and* get the ball," says Jane Kihlstrom, whose Bichon Riley holds all other flyball titles and is about to receive his Flyball Grand Champion title.

Kihlstrom notes that it's important for flyball dogs to be outgoing, confident, and well socialised, because the sport is held in close, loud quarters around lots of people and other dogs. Both Speedie and Kihlstrom didn't have to use any special methods to

Dress for Success — Flyball

Flyball clothes should be casual, comfortable, and suited to athletic activity, but neat. Some teams may wear uniforms or closely coordinated outfits.

Flyball is a fast-paced relay race that involves catching a ball and jumping over hurdles.

teach their Bichons, who were eager to play, but do recommend taking the training one segment at a time—catching the ball, jumping over hurdles, and so forth.

Spectators and handlers love the sport as much as the dogs. Speedie says Poppy loves her teammates, and Speedie herself enjoys being around other people who are as crazy about their dogs as she is about Poppy. Despite her love of the competition, Speedie says her focus is on having fun safely, being a good sport, and providing many dogs the opportunity to run.

"Flyball gives me a chance to have a blast playing with my dog. He loves to run," Kihlstrom says, "We spend the whole weekend together, and both come home with smiles on our faces."

If you think you and your Bichon would enjoy competing in Flyball, you can get more information from the Kennel Club (www.the-kennel-club.org.uk) and from the British Flyball Association (www.flyball.org.uk).

OBEDIENCE

Obedience on the competitive level takes the commands learned in a basic obedience class and puts them into a structured form, in which dog and handler are tested on their ability to receive and precisely execute these commands.

Like the Good Citizen awards, obedience titles signify a dog's ability to be well-trained and well-behaved at home and in public. Obedience competitions were originated to demonstrate the ability of dogs to be good companions to humans.

Dress for Success—Obedience

Clothes for Obedience should be tailored casual, but with room for adequate movement. Competitors often wear jeans and other weekend-style clothes, but overall appearance should make a neat impression. Shoes should be non-slip.

Dancing With Your Dog?

Dancing with dogs (known as canine freestyle) is not a movie spin-off but an activity in which owners and dogs spin around the dance floor together. Competitions involve the performance of original routines choreographed to music. Steps are loosely based on obedience-style movements incorporating dance steps with a creative flair. Owner and dog are in costumes that correspond with the theme of the music.

"Bichons do well with freestyle," Nancy Bayless says, "It incorporates their ability to learn and perform tricks and most of them like the attention from the audience."

Dogs and owners are judged on teamwork, creative artistry, style, interpretation, and athleticism. Demonstrations of this fun sport are supposed to be as enjoyable to an audience as to the participants. Freestyle is designed to demonstrate the joy of the human–dog bond, while both owner and dog have a good time competing for titles.

At a competition, dogs are placed in a class depending on previous wins, and must perform a set series of exercises. Starting with the six most basic commands, requested commands increase in difficulty with each level, including:

- Heelwork on lead.
- Heelwork off lead.
- Recall.
- Stays. This includes Sit-Stays and Down-Stays. In the higher classes the handler is out of sight.
- Retrieve. This may be a dumbell or an article chosen by the judge.
- Distance Control. The dog must go into the Sit, Stand and Down when commanded from a distance.
- Sendaway. The dog is directed to drop on command at a marker he is sent to.
- Scent discrimination. The dog picks out a cloth that has the scent of the handler or judge.

The highest title a dog can earn in the UK is Obedience Champion, which involves winning three Challenge Certificates (from Class C) under three different judges.

Is Obedience Right for Your Bichon?

In the US, Bichon owners have made their mark in competeitive obedience. "Many Bichons are not comfortable in the obedience ring, with all its formality," says Nancy Bayless, "But it can be done and there have been Bichons who were successful in the obedience ring."

Training and practice methods should be varied to better suit the Bichon personality and style of learning. "The training method I use is all positive (food motivated) and exaggerated," explains Rilda Fish, owner of Bichon Happy Go Ryelee CD, whose last leg towards his title was earned with a high score of 194, "I do a lot of confidence-building exercises."

Despite the stress that formal obedience might cause in some Bichons, others may do well. Their inclination to make direct eye contact results in great attention to commands, and their need to be close to their owners helps with heelwork. Because of their desire to please, using positive methods, some Bichons can be easily trained for the obedience ring.

If your Bichon has passed a basic obedience class with flying colours, it might be satisfying to see if you can earn an obedience title or two. "Why did I get involved in obedience with a Bichon of all dogs!? Because obedience has always interested me, and Genta showed an early talent for it," says Anita Lupcho of her dog, who is on his way to earning his Companion Dog title. "It was an opportunity to do something with a dog I love, and it's fun for both of us. Plus, I truly wanted to show that Bichons can do anything."

Obedience serves another purpose: If your Bichon is stressed or nervous about new or uncertain situations, working with you through obedience training or competition is a way to provide him with calming confidence. If you want to see if earning an obedience title is right—and fun—for you and your Bichon, join a training club, attend some competitions, and see how your dog responds.

The Bichon's inclination to make direct eye contact helps them pay attention to obedience commands.

RALLY OBEDIENCE

Rally-O is a brand new sport in the US, and is ideal for Bichons. It is similar to obedience, but is designed to be more relaxed and fun for both dog and owner. Dogs must still understand and respond to obedience commands, but competitions are not as formal and do not require as much precision.

Owners and dogs work their way through a course of stations. The stations have signs that instruct the handler what command should be performed next. The total number of stations and type of commands, which can include small jumps, are determined by class competition level, which are based on the dog and owner's past competitive history.

Unlike obedience, handlers may repeatedly use hand signals and talk to their dogs throughout the course to show them what actions they want them to perform. The use of encouragement and praise are actually promoted. Rally-O was designed to bridge the activity gap between completion of a CGC and formal obedience.

As Rally-O is a new sport, training and trials are just getting off the ground in the US. If it is successful, there is a good chance it will spread to the UK and will be recognised as a new discipline.

SHOWING (CONFORMATION)

As the name implies, conformation is an event that judges how

Dog shows judge how closely a dog conforms to the standard for his breed.

closely a dog—in this case a Bichon—conforms to the standard for his breed. The purpose of judging a dog against a standard is to help evaluate which dogs will best continue their breed by producing puppies.

But a dog show is much more than that. It's a beauty pageant, a muscle contest, and a beautiful spectator sport. It's a social event, a family event, and a bit confusing for those unfamiliar with the process.

Competition starts with experienced, educated judges who evaluate dogs in single-breed classes divided by gender and age. Handlers pose dogs in a stand for inspection of body structure and type, fur colour and texture, correct eyes, head, tail, bite, ear-set, and even temperament. The handlers then "gait" the dogs around the ring, individually. The handler may be asked to move the dog in a triangle, or straight up and down the ring, in order to demonstrate the motion appropriate to the breed.

Winners are selected from each class, then the best male and female are chosen from these selections. These dogs will be awarded with Challenge Certificates. The judge will then choose one dog as Best of Breed who will go forward to compete with all Best of Breed winners in the Toy Group. Then all Group winners (from the Toy, Hound, Terrier, Gundog, Working, Utility, Pastoral groups) will compete for the prestigious Best in Show

Good To Know

Bichons who might not like or respond well to the more rigid requirements of obedience may enjoy rally obedience, which is now taking off in the US.

award. This is awarded by a Best in Show judge, who will select the dog who most closely conforms to its breed standard on that day.

Getting Started

If you think you might like to show a dog, what does it take to get started? The process actually begins before you have a puppy. Future show dog owners must research the breed's standard, breeders, advertisements, pedigrees, and health histories before selecting a show prospect and making a purchase. Owners who wish to handle their own dogs must take handling classes and learn proper ring technique.

Additionally, the future show dog needs training before entering the ring. Handlers should start teaching young puppies to accept being groomed, posed, and inspected, and to being in noisy crowds around many dogs. Show dogs must be well nourished and placed on a regular exercise programme to build and maintain muscle. And that high-maintenance Bichon coat must be kept in perfect order at all times.

In addition to an exemplary dog and good handling, showing dogs in conformation requires a considerable commitment of time, money, and effort, day in and day out, weekend after weekend. Why is the effort worthwhile? In addition to bonding with your dog and having the satisfaction of earning your dog's title, conformation is important because it focuses on the continuation of healthy dogs who will make good companions, generation after generation.

Donna Jones, breeder of MusicBox Bichons, Oxford, Georgia believes the best reason to show in conformation—and the only reason to ever breed puppies—is to improve the breed and to have a great time with your dog.

Dress for Success— Conformation

Conformation is a more formal sport. Handlers should wear business dress: suits, matching or coordinated pant suits, or dresses, with plenty of pockets for bait and brushes. Choose colours that accent your dog's appearance but don't stand out. Clothing, while not sloppy, should allow free movement for bending down to the dog and for gaiting. Shoes should be comfortable and made for running but also not have a too-casual appearance.

Winning show dogs have outgoing personalities and are not nervous or fearful.

What Does It Take To Make a Show Dog?

Not every dog is born to become a show dog. What are the extras that make up a show-quality dog, a dog destined for the winner's circle? A show dog:

- Conforms physically to a detailed description of what an ideal Bichon should be;

- Has been planned for generations, before he was born, and has ancestors who are also show dogs;

- Is very healthy and in excellent condition;

- Has an outgoing personality and is not nervous, fearful, or dull;

- Is well-trained and well-mannered;

- Has confidence, and clearly says, "Look at me — I'm special!";

- Is a beloved companion to his owner.

Her advice is sound. Her dog (co-owned with Rick Day), CH Risgae's Wild Bill, was the third-ranked Bichon in the US for 2004, with a couple Best in Show wins to his credit.

If competing with your dog for these honours sounds like an activity you'd enjoy, research, study, watch, and learn everything you can about Bichons and shows from experts like breeders, handlers, and judges. "Go to all the dog shows you can attend, and chat with anyone that will talk to you about showing. Join and go to ringcraft classes" recommends Jones. Contact the Kennel Club (www.the-kennel-club.org.uk) for details.

Championships

In the United Kingdom, a dog must win three Challenge Certificates (CC) from three different judges, with one of these Certificates being awarded after the age of 1 year. To win a CC, a dog must already have been chosen for Best of Sex.

Although it sounds simple, earning the CC in the United Kingdom is not easy, because not all shows offer these certificates. CCs are allocated by the Kennel Club based on the popularity of the breeds being shown. Additionally, dogs who have already earned a CC can continue to compete for more certificates. It is not uncommon in KC shows for dogs who win frequently at the breed, group, and best-in-show level to never become Champions.

To earn an AKC Champion title, a dog must beat other dogs in multiple age and gender classes to become Winners Dog or Winners Bitch. Based on how many dogs are beaten, points, up to a maximum of five at one time, are earned. Some of the points won must be "majors," in which the dog earns three or more points in a single-breed class. A total of 15 points, with two majors, are necessary to become a Champion of Record.

A Canadian championship is earned when a dog is awarded a total of 10 points under three different judges. One of these wins must be worth at least two points, given at either the breed or group level.

THERAPY DOGS

A Bichon a day will keep the blues away, may be the motto of many an owner. Why not share some of that Bichon joy with others who are depressed, sick, or institutionalised? With their sweet, loving personalities and faces cute enough to drive away a bad day, many Bichons are ideal candidates for therapy dogs.

Therapy dogs are outgoing, well-mannered dogs who, with their owners, visit residents or patients in nursing homes, hospitals, and other care facilities where the people may be cheered or comforted by the temporary companionship of a friendly dog. The purpose of these visits is to improve the quality of life and health for these persons through friendly contact with an animal who relieves depression, reduces stress, and promotes health.

A number of recent scientific studies have shown that contact with a pet has significant health benefits. Stroking a cat or dog lowers the blood pressure and has a beneficial effect on the immune system. There are also benefits to a person's mental health. Studies demonstrate that people who have regular interaction with pets have much lower stress levels.

Nancy Rosen, owner of two Bichon therapy dogs, Maggie and K.C., describes the Bichon as a clean-looking dog with a friendly appearance who feels good to touch, making them ideal for this type of work. "They are a good size to hold or put in someone's lap or bed. But they aren't so small they are easily hurt," says Rosen, "Bichons are easy to train to do tricks, which can make therapy visits all the more enjoyable. People smile when they see them."

For those interested in doing therapy visits, Rosen recommends that owners socialise their Bichon in as many different situations as possible. Exposure to the types of sounds, equipment, furnishings, flooring surfaces, smells, and people they might encounter on visits is helpful. A good foundation in basic obedience training is necessary.

Conformation Eligibility

To compete in conformation dogs must:

- Be registered with the Kennel Club (or other relevant organisation);
- Not have any disqualifying faults according to the Bichon standard;
- Be a minimum age of 6 months;
- Be in mandated show trim;
- Cannot be spayed or neutered.

Therapy dogs bring comfort and companionship to many people, including residents of nursing homes.

Qualifications

In the UK, the governing body for therapy dogs is Pets as Therapy (PAT). For detailed information on registering your Bichon as a PAT dog, visit their website (www.petsastherapy.org).

A dog must be a minimum of 9 months of age before applying to be a therapy dog. A registered evaluator will check on the dog's general health and temperament. The dog will then be tested to see if he will walk on a loose lead, remain under control despite distractions, and not react to loud or sudden noises. The evaluator will also check to see if the dog is happy to be groomed, as this shows whether a dog will accept all over handling and touching. Once your dog is accepted to work as a PAT dog, you can approach local hospitals and care homes and make arrangements to start visiting.

FUN AND EXERCISE

All activity with your Bichon does not have to be structured or competitive. Some of the most fun you have may be playtime around the house or recreation outdoors.

Games

As long as you are playing with him, your Bichon will enjoy about any doggy type activity in which you engage. They like chasing balls, catch, playing with squeaky toys, and a good game of tag or chase. Bichons particularly seem to like to play hide and seek, which is also an excellent way to teach the Come command. Hide while your dog is not looking, then softly call him to come. When he finds you, give him a treat.

Bichons also like to search for hidden treats. Any game that utilises their sense of smell is fun

You can play many fun games in your own home with your Bichon.

for them. For nondominant dogs, a careful game of tug is also pleasurable entertainment. A football game you can try is to stand in a door and, using your foot, roll a ball toward your Bichon. When he tries to come through the doorway, roll the ball back away from him.

Bichons love to learn and perform tricks.

Some Bichon owners like to wrap a string around the neck of an empty, dry, plastic bottle. Your dog can grab the string and have fun dragging the toy around. The longer the string, the more the bottle bounces and the more fun your dog can have. If you have two dogs, one can pull while the other chases.

Tricks

Because of their ancestors' background as circus entertainers, many Bichons love to learn and perform tricks. Working from a base of the basic obedience commands, your Bichon can be taught to roll over, shake hands, and play dead. If he has a natural inclination to do the wave, teach him to dance. Some owners have taught their Bichons to put away their toys, play football, sneeze, whisper, and even bring the paper.

When combined with therapy visits, a performing Bichon will put a smile on many a face. There are a number of books available that suggest tricks for your dog to learn, along with step-by-step directions for teaching these tricks. Another resource is the Internet. You can correspond via e-mail with other Bichon owners about what methods they use to teach their dogs how to be canine superstar performers.

Walking and Hiking

Just about any dog loves to go for a walk. Get out a lead, put on your walking shoes, and most Bichons will be waiting eagerly at the door. With short little legs, it doesn't take long for a walk to turn into an endurance event, so plan on starting out small and work up to greater distances. Maximum distance for a Bichon usually shouldn't exceed 2 miles (3 km).

If 2 miles is long, then how can you hike with your Bichon? Take a back-pack carrier or puppy pouch. Most Bichons love to go on an outing in the woods with their person. With a carrier along, your dog can hike a bit, get carried a bit, then walk some more if he's able.

Be cautious about small feet picking up burrs, briars, and thorns, and little legs getting caught or twisted by tree roots and crevices between rocks. Carefully restrain your Bichon near the edge of any drops. Along with a carrier, take a hydration pack. Include enough water for both of you, a collapsible bowl for him, and a small snack or dry meal for day hikes.

On a hike or a walk, don't let your dog get too tired, but have fun getting some exercise together; it's healthy for both of you.

Bichons love attention, and some are even spiffy dressers.

Out and About

Bichons love to be made much of. Like most dogs, they also like to go for car rides. Put the two together, and you have the combination for fun on the run with your dog. Bichons are the perfect dog for going with you on errands to the shop. Most Bichons love the car so much they don't care if they stay put. It is enough to go on an outing with their beloved owner.

There are a limited number of shops that will allow dogs, such as hardware stores or some garden centres. Always check first and make sure your Bichon is on a lead and under control. And, of course, don't forget that friendly dogs on lead are usually welcome to shop at pet supply stores.

Local Bichon owners can arrange to get together for a mini-bash, to chat while their dogs have a play date. Any type of outing, like a trip to an outdoor ice cream stand or a jaunt in the park, is enjoyable for you and your dog, and an excellent way to have fun, teach him how to behave in public, and socialise him at the same time.

Just Being a Dog

Since Bichons are born and bred to be companions, some of the best times you can enjoy are when you and he do nothing but be together. The super-affectionate, extra-cuddly Bichon is perfect for an afternoon nap and snuggle. Make television time cuddle time, which will make you both happy. Even grooming, such a necessity with the Bichon, can be a special time for bonding, because the two of you are spending time focused solely on each other. Whatever task or activity you undertake together, enjoy the pleasure of each other's company. That's part of what loving a dog is all about.

HEALTH

of Your Bichon Frise

Many elements make for a healthy dog—genetics, diet, exercise, and environment—but following a strong preventive health care programme, along with monitoring for symptoms and seeking treatment as soon as your Bichon becomes ill, are key steps to giving him a life of wellness.

THE BEST VET FOR YOUR BICHON

One of the most important tasks an owner does for his dog is to provide regular, quality veterinary care. Find a veterinary surgeon who is knowledgeable, compassionate, and with whom you feel comfortable. Look close to home first, so you don't waste time getting to the clinic should an emergency arise. But don't be unwilling to drive further afield if the best vet is at a distance from your home.

Word of mouth is an excellent way to find a vet. Ask people who see many dogs, such as your groomer or training instructor, which vets have a reputation as skilled caregivers. Where do your friends take their dogs? What do they like about the vet, the clinic, and staff?

Take time to do as much research as possible. The vet is going to be a very important person in your Bichon's life, and you owe it to your dog—and yourself—to find a practice that is going to suit your needs.

Once you have narrowed your search, schedule an appointment to visit the clinic and meet the vet or vets in the practice. Find out if at least one vet has experience with small dogs (Bichons in particular) and is educated about conditions to which the breed is prone. Also, look for the following on your visit:

- Is the clinic clean?
- Do the staff seem helpful?
- Are the hours convenient and the fees reasonable for the services provided?
- Is the vet willing to talk to you, and are you able to understand what he or

Finding a vet you trust is the first step to your Bichon's good health.

she is telling you?

• Do you feel like you can build a working client–patient–doctor relationship?

Don't wait until you have a veterinary emergency to choose your vet. Finding a vet in whom you are confident enough to entrust your dog's care is not an easy task. Many questions must be asked and factors analysed in making your final decision. However, personal intuition is important as well. If you don't feel comfortable with a vet for any reason, keep looking; your dog's life may depend on your decision.

FIRST AND FUTURE EXAMS

It is important to schedule a veterinary exam for your new Bichon, ideally within 24 to 72 hours of bringing him home. This appointment also serves as an opportunity for your dog to meet his vet under less stressful circumstances than when being seen for medical treatment.

During the first visit, the vet will check your puppy for obvious congenital defects. He will perform a thorough physical examination, check for external parasites and advise on a worming programme. Your dog's history will be reviewed and recorded, and you can find out when vaccinations are due.

If you have questions about puppy care or behaviour, this is a good time to ask. Preliminary information about potential problems and procedures can be provided. You can also book an

First Vet Visit

On your first visit, the vet will do the following:

• Weigh the puppy.

• Check for worms.

• Examine his eyes, ears, mouth, teeth and gums, tongue, and throat.

• Palpate his abdomen for umbilical hernia, "pot belly," state of internal organs.

• Move and flex his joints through range of motion.

• Listen to his chest, heart, and lungs with a stethoscope.

• Evaluate his eating and elimination habits.

• Check his skin and coat condition.

• Evaluate his activity level.

appointment to start your puppy's vaccination programme.

Good health for a lifetime only starts with the first puppy visit. Besides a healthy lifestyle, your Bichon should have an annual veterinary check-up. This examination will be similar to the puppy examination. Additionally, any health problems that your dog might have developed will be monitored. Blood and urine samples may be taken, and possibly an X-ray. Medications, diets, and treatment plans, if needed, will be adjusted. If vaccinations are due, they can be given at this time.

Annual well-dog examinations are an excellent tool for diagnosing conditions that may just be surfacing. As your Bichon ages, special emphasis on preventive health care can give him a more comfortable, longer life with you.

VACCINATIONS

A large part of your dog's care is protection against fatal and life-threatening infectious disease through vaccination (immunisation against a virus). Originally given each year as part of the annual exam, vaccination protocols are currently being reconsidered by veterinary colleges and professional organisations. The possible association of disabling, chronic illness due to over-vaccination has been the main reason for this change.

It is still necessary for your dog to be vaccinated. Decide with your vet how often you will vaccinate and for which diseases. Vaccines for the most prevalent and potentially lethal diseases

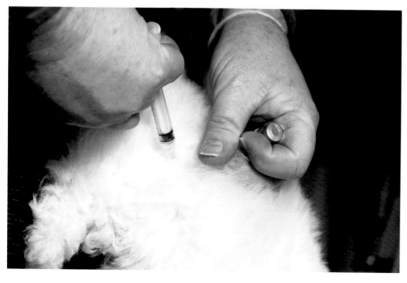

A large part of your Bichon's care is protection against fatal and life-threatening infectious disease through vaccination.

Dogs who participate in shows usually are immunised against Bordetella.

come either in combination for multiple viruses or individually.

Vaccines Your Bichon May Require

Corona

Corona is a virus that affects the gastrointestinal system and causes foul-smelling, bright yellow or orange diarrhoea. Other symptoms may include loss of appetite, depression, and vomiting. Most cases are mild, but puppies and debilitated dogs can become quite ill or even die. A vaccine is available and is recommended for dogs who are in frequent contact with other dogs. The schedule for this optional vaccine is to administer it in two doses 2 to 3 weeks apart. It is also available in a multicomponent vaccine.

Distemper

Extremely contagious, this virus affects the lining of many organs including the eyes, respiratory system, gastrointestinal system, and brain. Symptoms include fever, loss of appetite, dehydration, mucous discharge, hard calluses on the foot pads, vomiting, and diarrhoea. Infection leads to death in nearly all cases, with very few dogs making a full recovery from the disease. Puppies are vaccinated at about ages 8, 12, and 16 weeks.

Hepatitis

A virus that attacks the liver, kidneys, and lining of the blood vessels, hepatitis is transmitted through urine, faeces, and saliva. The disease takes multiple forms, ranging from mild to fatal, with symptoms that include high fever, loss of appetite, bloody vomit and diarrhoea, abdominal pain, and jaundice. Immunisations are given at 8 and 12 weeks of age.

Kennel Cough Complex

KCC is a group of highly contagious diseases that cause bronchitis and inflammation of the throat, resulting in a deep, spasmodic, hacking cough. The most common causes of KCC are the parainfluenza virus or the *Bordetella* bacteria. Both are easily spread through droplets sprayed during sneezing or coughing, and via contaminated bowls, bedding, and so forth. Both types of KCC are preventable through immunisation.

Parainfluenza vaccine can be administered in conjunction with distemper or hepatitis shots, or by intranasal spray as early as 2 weeks of age. The Bordetella bacterin (immunisation against a bacterial infection) is available for intranasal administration or as an injection.

Bordetella Immunisation

Immunisation against Bordetella is recommended annually for any dog who is frequently around other dogs, such as in a kennel or at a dog show.

Leptospirosis

This bacterial infection is transmitted in the soil, from wildlife, and through the urine of infected dogs. Lepto is more prevalent in some regions of the country than others. Multiple strains of leptospirosis occur, but the main symptoms are fever, lack of appetite, nausea and vomiting, and pain. Complications are common, and include kidney failure, liver damage, dehydration,

Your vet will know about the incidence of infectious diseases in your area.

internal bleeding and haemorrhage, and death. Immunisation can be done at ages 9, 12, and 15 weeks.

Lyme Disease

Lyme disease is rare in the UK, but its incidence is increasing. It can be transmitted if your dog is bitten by a deer tick. Symptoms of this chronic bacterial infection include depressed appetite, weight loss, lethargy, fever and, primarily, lameness and swollen joints. Possible development of arthritis and heart inflammation can occur. Immunisation is available against Lyme, but the efficacy is variable and is recommended only for dogs who live in areas with high tick infestation, such as parts of the USA.

Parvovirus

Another highly contagious virus, parvo is transmitted through faeces. The virus is difficult to kill and can be carried on clothing, feet, and fur, as well as living in contaminated crates, bedding, and bowls. Loss of appetite, profuse vomiting and diarrhoea (often bloody), and a high fever are the main symptoms. Puppies contract the disease most frequently and become severely ill or die, often within a few hours. Vaccination schedules for parvo vary, but should start at between 6 to 8 weeks of age and be given every 3 to 4 weeks, with a possible additional booster at either age 16 or 20 weeks.

Rabies

This is not applicable to dogs born in the UK, but it is important if you plan to take your dog overseas. Rabies is a fatal virus that attacks the nervous system and causes encephalitis. Rabies is transmitted in saliva from infected animals. Symptoms include personality changes, fever, aggression, salivation, paralysis, and death. Vaccination is done at age 3 months, 1 year, then every 3 years.

Vaccination Protocol

Based on a slowly growing body of evidence, an increasing number of vets recommend that booster immunisations be given every 3 years, instead of every year. Additionally, the criteria for determining which vaccines to administer are being evaluated. Vaccines have been divided into two groups: core and non-core vaccinations. Core vaccines are for diseases that are life-threatening or fatal if contracted. Non-core vaccinations are advised for dogs who have a greater than average risk of being exposed to the infectious agent, partially based on whether the region where they live has a high occurrence of a specific disease.

Based on your Bichon's health history and status, his activity type, involvement and contact with multiple dogs, and his risk of having an adverse or chronic reaction as the result of vaccination, your vet will recommend which vaccines he should receive and how often.

Vaccination Reactions

Immediate or Short-term

For a day or two after he has been vaccinated, it is possible for your dog to lose his appetite, be feverish and lethargic, and experience swelling or discomfort at the injection site.

More serious are allergic reactions which can be fatal. Symptoms of an allergic response are itching, hives, swelling of the face and head, vomiting, or diarrhoea. Allergic reactions can progress into *anaphylactic shock*. The symptoms of shock are the same as an allergic reaction but worse, and include swelling of the

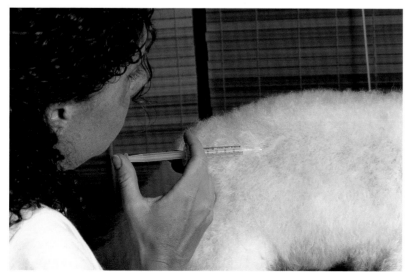

Your vet will recommend which vaccines your Bichon should receive and how often.

Spaying and Neutering

Neutering (or spaying) your Bichon means surgical sterilisation, which results in the inability to produce puppies. Besides preventing unplanned litters, sterilisation also prevents many types of cancer or diseases of the reproductive organs. And, most important, neutering reduces the pet population. As much as many people love and admire dogs, millions of unwanted, uncared-for dogs live in this world — even Bichons — and most end up euthanised for lack of a good home.

The huge majority of dogs should not be bred, including your own pet; most Bichons do not have what it takes to pass on good traits and genes to another generation. However, if you are hoping to be a breeder, do your homework! It will take years of study, research, showing, planning, and money (lots of money), to produce even one litter of healthy, quality Bichon pups.

Remember, dogs should only be bred for the betterment of the breed, not for profit. Have your Bichon sterilised.

eyelids, tongue and throat, fluid in the lungs, wheezing, difficulty breathing, restlessness, rapid heartbeat, collapse, convulsions, coma, and ultimately death.

Small dogs like the Bichon are more prone to allergic reactions. If your dog shows any of these symptoms within a few minutes or hours after receiving a vaccine, seek veterinary treatment immediately.

Delayed or Long-term

Another side effect from vaccination is the overstimulation of the immune system. This can result in autoimmune disease, in which the body attacks and destroys its own tissue. Vaccination-related autoimmune diseases can attack the joints, kidneys, blood or vascular system, the skin, nervous system, or gastrointestinal tract. Symptoms are widely varied.

Besides a misdirected immune system, the opposite is possible and resistance to other infectious diseases may be reduced. Some vets believe that recurring ear and bladder infections are a sign of this condition.

COMMON HEALTH ISSUES FOR THE BICHON

Every dog has its day, an old saying goes, and every breed has its own health problems. The Bichon is no exception to this adage, with a greater tendency than most other breeds to experience allergies, luxating patellas, bladder stones, and cataracts. Bichons also have a frequent occurrence of dental disease, pancreatitis, and anterior cruciate ligament (ACL) tears requiring repair.

"I believe the number one reason these problems are more common in the Bichon is because the breed has become much more popular over the last 10 to 15 years," says Dr. Larry Letsche, DVM, Remrock Farms Veterinary Services and also co-owner with his wife of Belle Creek Bichons, "With this increase in popularity, the number of puppies from people who only want to sell a litter and do zero genetic testing or planning before they breed has greatly increased."

Dr. Remrock suggests that the best way to prevent these problems is by purchasing your Bichon puppy from an ethical breeder who genetically tests her dogs and plans breedings with a strong eye to health histories.

Ethical breeders do their best to prevent health problems in their Bichons.

Allergies

Dr. Letsche notes that Bichons are considered to be one of the top 15 breeds to experience chronic skin allergies. An inherited predisposition is one component of allergies, but today's environment, with increased amounts of allergens and pollutants, is another likely culprit to bring on a case of the itchies. Various types of allergies occur: atopy—an inherited condition usually resulting in itchy skin; food allergies that may be related to inflammatory bowel disease; inhalant allergies that involve the upper respiratory system; and flea allergies that affect the skin. Although skin allergies may be triggered by an inhaled allergen, inhalant allergies that cause respiratory symptoms such as runny nose are not common in the Bichon.

The first sign that your Bichon may be suffering from allergies is frequent, repeated scratching, especially around the ears, muzzle, and shoulders, which can result in hair loss. Chewing and licking of the paws or the base of the tail, redness of the skin, and development of hot spots are additional signs. Fur around the mouth and those areas that your dog licks can discolour to a pinkish or ruddy brown shade.

Dogs can be allergic to many of the same things that humans are—dust, mould, pollen, and grass. Bichons also tend to be allergic to flea bites. Additionally, sensitivity to certain foods can be a problem for some Bichons. Food allergies can cause itchy skin, but also vomiting or diarrhoea. Allergens in food can be

Allergy Fact

Dogs can be allergic to dust, mould, pollen, grass, flea bites, and certain foods.

from proteins like beef, chicken, or dairy products; cereal grains like soy, corn, or wheat; and a vast array of additives (fillers, artificial colouring, flavouring, or preservatives).

Treatment

The first step in treatment is to consult your vet and consider allergy testing. Once the allergens are determined, eliminate or reduce exposure to them. Treatment is needed to break the itch-scratch-itch cycle. Antihistamines or corticosteroids may be prescribed alone or in combination, but be cautious in the usage of steroids, because they can have far-reaching side effects. Like people, dogs can also receive long-term treatments designed to desensitise them to allergens.

Supportive therapy between symptom flare-ups can ease the itch. Essential fatty acid supplements can help from the inside out by balancing and supporting the natural moisturising oils found in skin. Topically, shampoos formulated to ease itching due to allergies can be applied when you bathe your dog. If your vet recommends the use of a skin conditioning lotion or oil, ask for directions from your groomer for the best way to apply the product to prevent the development of mats, which can aggravate already irritated skin.

Food allergies are treated in a similar manner. Your dog must be on an elimination diet to find which ingredient is causing the allergic response. His diet may need modification, possibly by feeding special hypoallergenic products for a lifetime, to prevent re-exposure to the allergen. Medications for the skin manifestation of dietary allergies are the same.

Chronic gastrointestinal symptoms should be treated by your vet, who may use drugs to soothe the digestive tract and relieve vomiting or diarrhoea.

Lifestyle changes that control environment and diet are the cornerstones of containing allergies. Bichons with allergies tend to have them for life, so constant vigilance will be necessary to keep your dog comfortable and itch-free.

Cataracts

Veterinary research has pinpointed cataracts as an inheritable disease in the Bichon. They occur at a high rate in dogs whose breeders have not tested for nor bred away from the defect; however, cataracts are decreasing in frequency in Bichons who come from kennels where breeders are testing. Since up to one-quarter of Bichons are genetic carriers for cataracts, testing for eye defects is essential in breeding programmes.

Be sure to consult your vet if you suspect any eye problems in your Bichon.

About 10 percent of Bichons will be affected by cataract development at some time during their life. *Juvenile* and *senile cataracts* occur when the lens of the eye begins to become opaque due to a change in the composition or fibres of the lens. The opacity results in partial or total loss of vision. A dog with cataracts may act uncertain in new places, run into walls and sniff more when locating a toy or food, due to vision loss. Cloudiness or a blueish tint may be visible when looking at the eye.

Treatment

If you suspect your dog is developing a cataract, consult your vet. In some cases, a referral to a veterinary ophthalmologist will be needed.

Various surgical techniques are available for removing cataracts, including aspiration, laser, and lens replacement, which allows a return to nearly normal vision. It is imperative that dogs who have had cataract surgery have their activity level temporarily reduced and be kept from scratching at their eye so that proper healing can take place.

Cataract Fact

About 10 percent of Bichons will be affected by cataract development at some time during their life.

Cataracts may also be caused by diabetes, inflammation of the eye, nutritional deficiencies, and injury, although cataracts in the Bichon are usually inherited. Prevention of cataracts is best done by avoiding the breeding of affected dogs, and by having a dog's eyes tested annually.

Test Alert

Breeding stock must always be checked for incidence of cataracts in their pedigree.

Cushing's Syndrome

In Cushing's syndrome, also known as hyperadrenalcorticism, the adrenal glands produce too much of the hormone cortisol. Normally a condition that occurs with aging, the Bichon is no more prone than other breeds to Cushing's, but does seem to develop the syndrome frequently. One possible reason for its occurrence in the Bichon is the common use of cortisone to help control the breed's allergy symptoms.

Middle-aged or veteran dogs are most likely to develop Cushing's. Symptoms often mimic those of other diseases, but dogs with the syndrome can be weak or lethargic, with slow heartbeat and lower-than-normal body temperature. Sick dogs may also experience lack of appetite, vomiting, weight loss, increased thirst and urination, and hair loss.

The diagnosis is made by testing adrenal hormone levels. Dogs with Cushing's need lifelong monitoring and treatment with special drugs that help maintain correct cortisol hormone balances.

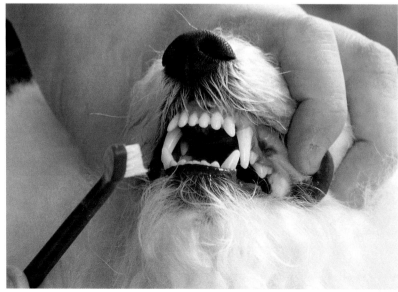

The best way to prevent dental disease is through regular teeth cleaning.

Dental Disease

Tooth loss due to deformity, gingivitis, premature decay, or retained baby teeth is not uncommon in toy-size dogs like the Bichon. Symptoms of dental problems include bad breath, red or swollen gums, bleeding, reluctance to chew or to eat hard food, food left around the gums and teeth after eating, and pain. Some situations, like retained baby teeth, warrant surgical intervention to remove the affected tooth or teeth.

Gingivitis, the inflammation of the gums caused by a build-up of tartar and plaque, can lead to deterioration of the bone beneath the teeth, which can also result in tooth loss. Additionally, bacteria that grows in the inflamed and decaying tissue can circulate through the body and cause disabling or life-threatening disease or dysfunction to develop in the heart, kidneys, or liver.

Prevention through regular teeth cleaning is the best treatment. Ask your vet to scale the teeth to remove plaque and tartar. Antibiotics may be administered prior to this thorough cleaning to prevent the possibility of serious infection.

Inflammatory Bowel Disease

Inflammatory bowel disease (IBD), not to be confused with irritable bowel syndrome, is a condition that sometimes occurs with long-term food allergies, a condition not uncommon in the Bichon. IBD has other causes but, in the Bichon, a food-related trigger is likely.

IBD may develop gradually or come on suddenly with episodes of explosive diarrhoea, often containing mucous or blood; vomiting, sometimes containing blood; loss of appetite; weight loss; urgent need to defaecate; straining; increased frequency of bowel movements; abdominal tenderness; and possibly a hunched position when standing or sitting.

Testing and treatment can be prolonged and prone to trial and error. Elimination diets are necessary to determine which foods are allergens. A vet may try a variety of medications, including those that coat and soothe the intestinal tract to relieve inflammation, or immune-suppressant drugs, as well as antibiotics specifically for

the gastrointestinal tract.

Once IBD has developed, and treatment has the worst symptoms under control, strict maintenance of a special diet is usually required for a lifetime. Some owners report success using raw diets for the IBD-affected Bichon. For more information on feeding, see Chapter 4.

Luxating Patellas

A technical name for slipped kneecap, patella luxation is the number-one orthopaedic problem in the Bichon. Occasionally, the condition is a result of trauma, but in the majority of cases, this congenital disorder is hereditary. The femur (long thigh bone) develops abnormally, which in turn pulls on the thigh muscle that is attached to the patella (kneecap). This causes the bones and ligaments of the knee joint to be misaligned and become deformed. Additionally, it is possible that the groove in the thigh bone, which holds and aligns the kneecap, is not sufficiently deep to prevent improper movement out of the joint.

The problem usually appears midway between puppyhood and adulthood, or in young adult dogs. If your dog has a luxating patella, he may skip sometimes instead of walking, with intermittent periods of lameness or pain. He may stop and stretch his leg out behind him in an attempt to get the kneecap to slip back into place. As the condition worsens, your dog may walk in a crouched position. Arthritis can develop in the affected joint.

Treatment

There are varying degrees of patella luxation. The least is a subluxated patella, which indicates a mild tendency to weakness and limited episodes of temporary misalignment. In most instances, the kneecap returns to proper position on its own. Because no long-term damage occurs to the joint, treatment is normally not necessary for subluxation. Care should be taken to prevent obesity or forms of exercise that can further strain the joint.

All other degrees of luxation, labeled grades 2, 3, or 4, indicate a condition that will worsen with normal usage of the leg. Surgery is the treatment of choice to repair and realign the joint. If you suspect your Bichon may have a luxating patella, don't put off getting veterinary attention. The sooner treatment is provided, the less damage and pain your dog will endure.

Bichons who are prone to patella luxation should be kept from jumping off high objects, like grooming tables. Ramps to get on and off beds or furniture may also slow the progression of joint and leg damage.

Otitis

In the Bichon, those cute floppy ears filled with fuzzy, curly fur are the perfect design for ear infections. The dog's ear anatomy in combination with a secondary condition (moisture, excessive wax, bacteria, yeast) can result in the development of otitis (inflammation or infection of the ear). Allergies, a big problem for the Bichon, are a prominent reason.

In addition to keeping the ear canal open by removing excess fur (see more in Chapter 5), keeping the ear clean helps reduce the possibility for infection. But don't be overzealous in wax removal, because water in the ear can cause infection too.

Symptoms of otitis are shaking of the head, frequent scratching at the ears, holding the head at an angle, redness of the skin on the ear flap, a foul odour from the ear canal, and the presence of dark brown, thick wax. Your veterinary surgeon can clean the ear and

ACL Repair

The ACL—anterior cruciate ligament—is a connective tissue in the knee. It helps hold the knee in correct position and maintains proper position during movement. In Bichons with luxating patellas, even low grade, the likelihood of a damaged ACL is increased.

Signs of ACL damage are pain, limping, and reluctance to put weight on the leg when standing or walking. Diagnosis is made when the vet moves the joint forward and backwards and finds it unstable. Surgical repair is necessary. Untreated ACL tears can result in scar tissue, painful arthritis, and a loss of mobility.

Reduce ACL problems by keeping your dog at his ideal weight and monitoring exceptionally energetic play, particularly if evidence of patella luxation is present.

If your Bichon has an ear infection, your vet will show you how to care for and clean the ear.

show you how to clean it at home during an infection. Antibiotic ointment or drops may also be prescribed.

Pancreatic Disease

Although no more common than in other breeds, the Bichon is frequently bothered by two diseases involving the pancreas.

Diabetes

Diabetes is a disease that results in an increased level of glucose (sugar) in the blood, caused by a decrease of the pancreatic production of insulin, a hormone that allows glucose to be broken down and absorbed by tissues for energy.

Signs of diabetes include increased thirst and urination, increased appetite, hyperactivity or lethargy, and weight gain. As the condition progresses, appetite may decrease and weight loss may occur. Uncontrolled diabetes can cause kidney damage, loss of vision, loss of circulation to the extremities, and more. High levels of blood sugar can lead to a build-up of ketones (a by-product of fat metabolism that increases as glucose metabolism decreases) which can cause nausea, vomiting, laboured breathing, lethargy, coma, and death.

Dogs with diabetes should be under ongoing veterinary care. Diagnosing diabetes is based on the results of basic blood and urine tests. At home, owners must learn to administer insulin, test blood sugar levels on a regular basis, and carefully monitor the diet and their dog's weight.

Pancreatitis

Pancreatitis is the sudden inflammation and swelling of the pancreas. It can occur at any age in the adult dog, but more often affects dogs ages 6 years or older.

Dogs who are overweight, on cortisone therapy (as for allergies), or have thyroid dysfunction or diabetes are prone to pancreatitis. Symptoms may sometimes be vague and nonspecific, but can include vomiting; loss of appetite; abdominal pain that causes panting, restlessness, and a hunched position; diarrhoea; fever; vomiting; weakness; and even shock or collapse.

Pancreatitis can be serious, and it can cause dangerous complications that may lead to death. Treatment for pancreatitis should be sought promptly. A mild case often resolves in a few

Did You Know?

Pancreatitis can occur at any age in the adult dog, but more often affects dogs ages 6 years or older.

days with medications to treat the symptoms. More serious cases usually require hospitalisation, IV (intravenous) fluids and electrolytes, close monitoring, and intervention with life-saving measures if necessary. Until recovery is complete, food is withheld.

Once a dog has had pancreatitis, the chance of a recurrence is increased. Dogs who recover from acute pancreatitis must be maintained on a fat-restricted diet. They should also be checked periodically for the development of diabetes.

Pyodermas

Pyodermas are skin infections that usually appear concurrent with allergies.

Acral Lick Granuloma

Differing from hot spots, lick granulomas result from chronic licking and take weeks or months to develop. They may be dry as opposed to the moist discharge that hot spots have. Causes in the Bichon are usually related to allergies, but can be due to stress. Treatment should address the underlying problem, relieve the itching due to allergy and prevent the dog from chewing on the lesion.

Lick granulomas may also have a behavioural aspect. Once a dog has repeatedly licked an area, the need to do so becomes compulsive. Separation anxiety may be associated with this behaviour. Dogs must be distracted to another activity when they start to lick the lesion. Vets may also prescribe drugs that block or alter the way the nerve endings in the area perceive discomfort or itching. Antibiotics and anti-compulsive medications are also very important for treating this problem.

Folliculitis

With chronic allergies, all the scratching and inflammation can often lead to a secondary infection. The organisms that cause these infections include yeast, staph, or various other bacteria.

Folliculitis causes the formation of small pimple-like bumps around the fur, usually on the abdomen and up the chest. Some bumps may crust, and the hair may look dull

Emu Oil

Emu oil is a natural food by-product, obtained when red meat from emus (a large bird similar to an ostrich) is processed. It is rich in fatty acids and is reputed to be useful in healing problematic skin conditions.

and patchy. To treat folliculitis, a culture swab may be taken by the vet to determine which antibiotic to prescribe. Allergies must be treated, and baths with medicated shampoo should be given several times over a period of a few weeks.

Hot Spots

Along with allergies comes repeated scratching, licking, and biting that can result in traumatic damage to the skin. These damaged, red areas are devoid of hair, with thickened skin, and an oozing, pus-like surface. Known as "hot spots," or acute moist dermatitis, these lesions are painful and tend to develop quite rapidly.

Treatment begins with controlling the underlying cause. In Bichons, this usually means treating allergies. Fur around the lesion should be clipped and the area cleansed with an antiseptic shampoo. An astringent is used to dry the lesion, then a combination antibiotic and steroid cream is applied for several days. Pain at the site may be severe enough to warrant sedation or anaesthesia during treatment. In some cases, oral antibiotics and steroids may be required to facilitate complete healing.

Some Bichon owners report that applying a medicated powder, followed by emu oil when a hot spot first begins to develop, helps prevent the lesion from fully forming. Others believe they have achieved positive results by cleansing the hot spot with hydrogen peroxide, then placing corn starch on it. Before trying these measures at home, consult with your vet.

Tear Stains

Like many white dogs, the Bichon is disposed to tear stains around his eyes. Stains range in colour from a pinkish-red to a rusty-brown. Staining may be caused in part by excess tearing. Allergies may cause excess tearing, and the round-shaped eyes for which the Bichon standard calls can cause tears to spill over the lower lids. The eyelid may roll inwards, or extra eyelashes may be present to irritate the eye, causing it to water. Eye infections can be another culprit for staining, as can too-small or blocked tear ducts.

The first step to controlling tear stains is to have your dog's eyes examined by a vet. If a mild or subclinical infection exists, antibiotic eye ointment or oral antibiotics may help. In chronic situations, a liquid antibiotic can be added to drinking water 5 days out of each month. If the tearing is a result of malfunctioning or defective tear ducts, a procedure can be done to unblock them.

When allergies are the cause, controlling allergy symptoms can help reduce tear staining. Bichons with food allergies may tear-stain, but finding a diet free of the ingested allergen may reduce the staining. Avoiding dog foods that contain artificial colours, particularly red, may help. A tendency to tears that stain may be genetic, because some Bichons with allergies or eye problems that cause excess tearing do not stain around their eyes.

Some owners have found a small, daily serving of yogurt helps. (Check with your vet to make sure that yogurt is all right for your dog.) Some owners provide their dogs with bottled or filtered water to reduce excess iron consumption, which can also sometimes cause tears to discolour the face.

For more information on cleaning tear stains from the face, see Chapter 5.

Urolithiasis

Bichons experience a higher than average occurrence of urinary stones, primarily in the bladder. Dr. Letsche notes, "There is a genetic link to this disease."

Urine contains waste products, many of which are minerals. Under normal conditions, these waste products dissolve. In urolithiasis, these products instead clump together into tiny crystals. These crystals remain in the urinary tract and form a

Two types of stones commonly afflict the Bichon—struvite and calcium oxalate.

framework upon which a stone eventually develops.

Stones, which vary in size, composition, and number, may impede or block urinary flow. In the early stages of development, stones may not cause noticeable symptoms, but most dogs eventually show signs of frequent urination, straining to urinate, urinating small amounts off and on over a period of time, dribbling, having "accidents," or passing blood in the urine.

If the urinary flow is completely blocked, this is an emergency. Signs of this critical condition may include nausea, vomiting, pain, whimpering or moaning, and distention of the bladder. Seek treatment immediately, because this condition can cause renal failure and death

Struvite Stones

Two types of stones commonly afflict the Bichon—struvite and calcium oxalate. Struvites, composed of magnesium ammonium phosphate, can become quite large and are more prevalent in females and dogs aged 2 to 5 years. Formation can be triggered by urinary tract or bladder infections (UTIs), another frequent problem in the Bichon, or alkaline urine (urine should have a slightly acidic pH). Diets high in cereal protein, like soybean or corn gluten, can contribute to struvite formation.

It is possible to dissolve some struvite stones through the use of medications, but surgery may be needed in some cases. Additionally, antibiotics may be administered to eliminate any present UTIs. Urinary acidifiers are given along with a prescription diet designed to maintain the proper urine pH. Once a dog has been diagnosed with and treated for stones, a modified diet, early treatment of UTIs, and monitoring of urine pH will be needed for his lifetime to prevent recurrence, which can happen in about 20 to 25 percent of affected dogs.

Calcium Oxalate Stones

Calcium oxalate are stones formed from a combination of calcium and oxalates, which come from products containing oxalic acid. These stones are usually smaller in size but occur in greater quantities. Causes are many and relate to varying changes and abnormalities in body and urine chemistry.

Older dogs, dogs with excessively high or low levels of calcium in their diet, high blood levels of calcium from other diseases, and male dogs are at greater risk of forming these stones. Hormonal changes or imbalances are another factor, as are obesity or diets containing too much vitamin C or D.

No medication is available to dissolve these stones, so surgery or a mechanical removal technique (urohydropropulsion) is necessary. A prescription diet with reduced sodium should be fed following removal. Additional follow-up treatment may include urinary alkalisers or diuretics. Urinary acidifiers should not be used, and medications containing cortisone should be avoided except on your vet's advice and under special circumstances.

Cal-ox stones have a high rate of recurrence, about 25 to 50 percent. To help reduce the chances, avoid feeding preserved meats (ham, bacon, etc.) or fish, broccoli, carrots, dairy products, and some fruit and grains. Do not supplement the diet with vitamins C or D.

Aftercare

After treatment for either type of stone, periodic urinalyses are necessary to check urine pH and detect the presence of crystals, infection, or blood in the urine. New drug protocols are being tested for treating stones, so ask your veterinary surgeon about all medication options. For Bichons with chronic bladder infections, cranberry extract supplements can be given to help reduce infection frequency, but check with your vet before adding them to your dog's diet.

Dogs who are prone to stone formation should be provided with frequent opportunities to empty their bladders. Exercise can also help the condition. A dog who is inactive or confined frequently for long periods will have more highly concentrated urine, which provides an environment that allows stones to form.

Increased water consumption is important for managing urolithiasis. For dogs who don't like to drink much, give them canned food, put water on their dry food, and offer popsicles or ice cubes to increase their water intake. The best way to prevent any stone is through the consumption and elimination of water.

Who's at Risk?

Some dogs are at a greater risk for forming calcium oxalate stones. They include:
- Veteran dogs
- Dogs with excessively high or low levels of calcium in their diet
- Dogs with high blood levels of calcium from disease
- Males

PARASITES

No one likes to think of their dog nurturing little creatures of his own, but it's all too common for dogs to be prone to infestation with parasites, both internal and external. Quite often, they are so common that owners take their existence for granted and overlook the health problems parasites can cause.

External Parasites

Fleas

"My dog has fleas," may be music to an in-tune ukulele, but it's not a refrain any dog owner wants to hear. With warm weather or outdoor play, the chance of your dog getting fleas is quite high if he and his environment are unprotected.

For Bichons, fleas aren't just a pest, they are the bearers of bad bites. Bichons are very prone to allergic reactions to flea saliva, which is injected into the dog's skin when they are bitten. Flea allergy dermatitis (FAD) causes extreme itching, scratching, and chewing. A rash or red, pimple-like bumps develop, which may ooze and scab, causing hot spots to develop.

FAD is treated by getting rid of the fleas on the pet and from the environment, bathing the dog, and applying a soothing spray. Dietary supplementation with fatty acids also helps. An antihistamine or corticosteroid may be administered by your

Check your Bichon for fleas after he's been outside.

veterinary surgeon to stop the allergic reaction.

Prevention. The most important way to treat flea bites is to prevent fleas. At the start of flea season, apply a topical spot-on treatment if your Bichon is not allergic to the product. Spot-ons work by killing adult fleas and interrupting the growth cycle (IGRs) of developing fleas. Dogs who are sensitive to spot-ons, which remain active in the skin for 3 to 4 weeks, may need to be dipped in a special flea-killer by your vet.

If neither of these are options for your Bichon, ask about a preventive spray that can be applied lightly to the coat a few times weekly, prior to going outdoors. Monthly oral preventives are not recommended for the hypersensitive Bichon, because it is necessary for the flea to bite the dog for the product to work, thus allowing the opportunity for FAD to occur.

Flea Shampoo. If your dog already has fleas, detected by black flecks in the fur and signs of bites, bathe him in hypoallergenic flea shampoo recommended by your vet. A water-based spray containing IGRs and made from permethrins or pyrethrins can be applied afterward. You must wait 48 hours before applying a topical, 30-day spot-on treatment.

Treat the Outside. Outside, flea havens must be cleaned and treated. Remove dead leaves, grass, pine needles, or other organic matter. Fleas thrive in the shady, moist environments under these materials. Apply a pesticide weekly for 3 weeks by diluting with water and spraying. Permethrin or chlorpyrifos are some chemicals suggested by professionals as either less harmful to pets or more effective against fleas.

Treat the Inside. Indoors, vacuum all carpets and upholstered furniture, and wash all bedding. Sodium polyborate powder can then be applied to carpeted areas. This flea eliminator is purported to have no toxicity and be effective for almost a full year.

Surfaces may also be sprayed with products containing IGRs, or with pesticides made from chrysanthemums and labeled as pyrethrins (natural form) or permethrins (synthetic form), which are also effective and safer for pets than indoor chemical insecticides containing organophosphates or carbamates.

Combining chemicals can be a recipe for a sick dog. For the safest recommendations on complete flea removal and control, consult your veterinary surgeon.

Flea Fact

Fleas, if swallowed, can cause tapeworm infestation. Long-term flea infestation can result in anaemia, which can be serious, even deadly, in small puppies.

Mange (Mites)

Three types of mange occur in dogs, all caused by a different mite and each having a predilection for attacking various areas of the body. *Sarcoptic mange*, also known as *scabies*, can be passed to humans. It is usually contracted by dogs living in dirty conditions. Puppies are most often affected by the other types of mange, *demodectic* and "walking dandruff" or *cheyletiellosis*. Dogs with demodectic mange seem to have a genetic predisposition to being affected by the mite, but the condition is uncommon in Bichons.

Mange can cause itching, oozing lesions, scabbing, hair loss, and damage to the skin. An appropriate topically safe insecticide must be applied to kill the mites. Oral medications may be given to help relieve itching and promote healing.

Ticks

It's been said before: Ticks are blood suckers. Dog ticks, deer ticks, and more, ticks are nasty little parasites that live on common wildlife and in brushy woods. To feed, they attach to a dog in hidden places like behind the ears, in the armpits, or on the inside of the legs. Ticks get larger as they become engorged with blood. Not only are they so small they're hard to find, they are hard to kill because of their tough exterior shell.

Ticks aren't just an inconvenience; they are carriers of very serious diseases. Dogs are susceptible to a variety of tickborne infections that are difficult to diagnose and treat. These debilitating diseases often induce a critical anaemia, can result in permanent damage to joints, or a chronic disease state. Many cases can be fatal or cause life-threatening heart, kidney, or liver damage.

Prevention is the best approach to tick management. Keep areas where your dog plays outside mowed and clear of fast-growing

Prevention is the best approach when dealing with tick management.

weeds. Use a flea preventative that incorporates a tick repellant or insecticide. If your dog does get a tick, carefully remove it with a pair of tweezers and thoroughly cleanse the bite with alcohol. Follow-up cleaning can be done with a little hydrogen peroxide on a cotton-wool ball.

The chances of your dog getting a tickborne disease are rare in the UK, but owners should be vigilant and seek veterinary attention if there is any sign of sickness after removal of a tick.

Internal Parasites

Intestinal and other internal parasites, although enough to make an owner's stomach turn, are not terribly uncommon, with most dogs having worms at some point in their lives. Many puppies are born with worms, even when the dam appears parasite free or has been wormed prior to conception. Except for heartworms, worms

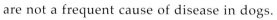

are not a frequent cause of disease in dogs.

As a matter of good health, internal parasites should be prevented, and infestations should be treated. Some worms can infest humans, causing disease. If symptoms cause you to suspect worms, take a sample of your dog's stool to the vet for analysis and to receive the correct deworming medications. In some cases, the vet may require a stool sample when giving the dog its annual check up.

Diseases From Ticks

Diseases that dogs can get from ticks are caused either by a protozoan (a single-celled microorganism that can cause disease) or a rickettsial bacteria. Treatment for tick-induced diseases usually consists of multiple, long-term antibiotic therapy plus other medications to treat additional symptoms, including anti-inflammatories and transfusions if severe anaemia ensues.

- **Lyme disease.** Fever, lameness, swollen joints; may be chronic; may affect nervous system, heart, and kidneys. Becomes chronic.

- **Ehrlichiosis.** Loss of appetite, lethargy, stiff achy muscles and joints, upper respiratory symptoms; chronic phase with weakness, swelling, enlarged spleen, bone marrow suppression and anaemia, organ failure. High rate of fatality.

- **Rocky Mountain Spotted fever.** Lethargy, inflammation of the eye, fever, inappetence, coughing, shortness of breath, vomiting or diarrhoea, swelling, staggering gait, seizures; chronic phase with bleeding disorders, haemorrhaging, blood in urine or faeces, organ failure; death is possible.

- **Babesiosis.** May not produce symptoms, but can be severe when symptoms are present, including anaemia and destruction of red blood cells, enlarged spleen and liver, fever.

Heartworms

These worms are rarely found in the UK, but they are present in most of the US. Heartworms are transmitted to a dog through the bite of infected mosquitoes. Once infected, the worm's larvae travel through the blood to the right chamber of the dog's heart, where they take about six months to mature. Signs of heartworm infection are coughing, (sometimes bloody), weakness, shortness of breath, exercise intolerance, and lethargy. By the time symptoms are present, heartworm disease is well advanced. Permanent heart damage or disease is possible, as is death.

If you live in an affected area, your Bichon will need a blood test every spring to test for the presence of heartworm microfilaria. The dog should then be placed on a preventive to keep him from getting this life-threatening parasite. An additional benefit of giving heartworm preventive is that it also helps prevent most other types of worms.

Hookworms

These small, narrow worms fasten to the small intestine. They are found in soil and the faeces of infected animals. Puppies may show signs of severe infestation, which includes anaemia and bloody diarrhoea. In long-term infection, or in adult dogs, symptoms also include diarrhoea and anaemia, plus weight loss and weakness.

Roundworms

Nearly every puppy is born with roundworms. Post-natal worming is routine for this type of helminth (parasitic worm). Older dogs get roundworms from ingesting soil contaminated with the eggs. The roundworm moves through various body systems as it develops from egg into adult and, at different stages, it can be found in the stomach, intestines, lung, organ or muscle tissue, and even the breast milk of dams. Signs of infestation include a potbelly, dull coat, failure to thrive, gagging cough, vomiting (sometimes of worms), and even death in young puppies. Worms may also be present in the stool. These are several inches long and resemble motile spaghetti.

Tapeworms

The head of this nematode attaches by suckers and hooks to the wall of the dog's intestine to draw nutrients. This type of worm develops in segments and can grow to several feet in length. Segments of the body, which contain eggs, are passed in your dog's faeces and can be seen there, or around his anus, looking like moist, mobile grains of cooked rice. Later, after they have been shed, they appear as dried rice grains.

Tapeworms may cause mild symptoms of diarrhoea, loss of appetite, and weight loss. Coat condition may also be negatively affected by tapeworm infestation. In addition to fleas, dogs can acquire tapeworms from eating wild animals that they have killed. A prescription medication is necessary to eradicate the tapeworm and the head from which it grows.

Whipworms

Whipworms are about 2 inches long and resemble a whip. Adult worms fasten to the wall of the large intestine. Dogs become infected from soil contaminated with worm

Threadworms

Another small worm, this helminth lives in contaminated soil or faeces, and the larvae sometimes enters the body through the skin. If signs are noticeable, they include watery diarrhoea and symptoms of lung infection.

eggs. Symptoms of infestation include diarrhoea, weight loss, and an unhealthy appearance. It may be necessary to examine multiple stool samples to confirm the presence of whipworms.

HOLISTIC AND ALTERNATIVE HEALTH CARE

Veterinary medicine, like human medicine, has kept pace with technology. More high-tech diagnostic testing and treatments are available for dogs than ever before. But like human medicine, veterinary medicine also has areas where technological advancement has not been able to increase a cure rate or raise the level of health, mostly with chronic conditions

Holistic health care places an emphasis on balance and encompasses a combination of traditional and alternative medicines.

where symptoms can linger for a lifetime.

In a search for treatments that can improve a dog's quality of life in chronic disease states, many owners have turned to alternative treatment methods. These approaches incorporate a variety of ancient and new, novel approaches. Holistic health care places an emphasis on balance, and it encompasses a combination of traditional and alternative medicines. It aims at treating the whole dog, not just the illness or injury, while reducing the stress and discomfort of treatment. Practitioners view the canine patient with compassion and respect, and choose techniques that maximise effectiveness, minimise harm, and are the least invasive.

"A truly holistic view involves looking at all options and choosing what works best with the fewest side effects," describes Dr. Shawn Messonnier, DVM, veterinary practitioner and columnist of *The Holistic Pet*, "I'm a conventional doctor by training, and I use conventional therapies in my practice. Whenever possible, I like to integrate as many different therapies as possible, since the best results in my practice tend to occur when conventional therapies are combined with complementary therapies. The holistic approach looks at all treatment options and chooses what works best for each patient."

Modalities considered can include chiropractic, acupuncture, homeopathy, herbal medicine, acupressure, massage, magnetic therapy, flower essences, crystals, energy healing, diet, and nutritional supplements. Brief descriptions of the more commonly used methods follow.

Acupuncture

The philosophy behind acupuncture puts forth that disease is caused by an imbalance of energy in the body. Treatment consists of placing in the body very fine needles at specific points, believed to be energy points and lines, to redirect and rebalance the energy. Stimulation of these points results in actual physiological and biochemical changes that produce a healing effect. Acupuncture treatment may produce mild discomfort, but is well tolerated by most dogs.

This method has been used on animals for at least 4,000 years

to help relieve pain and treat musculoskeletal disorders, nervous disorders, and diseases of the urinary tract, gastrointestinal tract, respiratory system, and skin. Ask your vet for assistance in locating a certified veterinary acupuncturist.

Acupressure and Massage

Acupressure is similar to acupuncture in philosophy and the treatment of specific points, but no needles are used. In many cases, acupuncturists can also do acupressure. A trained massage therapist can sometimes do acupressure. Pet massage has become a popular way to assist in the healing of injuries or disorders of the musculoskeletal system, reduce stress, and relieve pain. Ask your vet for a referral. Books on pet massage are also available to help you learn some techniques for use at home.

Chiropractic

People have been receiving chiropractic treatment—the gentle manipulation of the spine and skeletal system—for decades. Now trained veterinary chiropractors are available to help dogs. Chiropractic works on the theory that the body must be in correct alignment to function properly.

Subtle movements in the joints or spine, caused by accident, stress, abrupt movement, athletic activity, or injury, can result in the misalignment of the skeletal structure and the simultaneous disruption of signals through the nervous system to the affected area. Treatment, which does not produce discomfort, returns the body to proper alignment and can help alleviate pain associated with the inciting condition.

Herbal or Botanical Medicine

The use of herbs to treat disease has been around as long as humans have been getting sick. Because dogs manifest disease in a similar manner, herbs used to treat people can be used to medicate dogs. Herbal preparations are made from different parts of a plant—roots, leaves, or buds—and are biochemically active. Many of today's drugs are derived from plants.

Because of their chemical properties, herbs can be used like drugs to treat many conditions. They can also have side effects and interact with other medications or herbs. If you wish to seek herbal treatment, consult a vet who is experienced in this practice. In general, herbs act more slowly and gently, and can be helpful in the treatment of chronic symptoms.

Homeopathy and Flower Essence Therapy

In traditional medicine, medicine is a weapon in the battle of illness against which the patient fights. The principle in homeopathy is that like cures like. Developed in the 1800s, after much scientific research by its founder, homeopathy treats by using remedies that, in healthy individuals, would cause the symptoms of a certain disease.

Remedies, which are the energetic essence of the disease state they seek to cure, are derived from plant, mineral, animal, bacterial, viral, or naturally occurring chemical sources. Flower essences, originally created by a homeopathic practitioner, are remedies made from flowers and targeted to work on the mind or emotions. Ask your vet for a referral to a specialist homeopathic vet.

Nutritional Therapy and Supplements

The first place to start treating many diseases is with a special diet, as you would for diabetes. These foods should be convenient to use, appeal to your dog, and be free of possibly harmful additives like artificial preservatives, flavours, or colouring. Supplements such as vitamins, minerals, amino acids, fatty acids, and other nutrients can be given to support specific organs, tissues, or body systems during recovery and after illness, to maintain health and prevent problems from recurring. Consult with your vet about prescribed diets, or with a veterinary nutritionist.

"Because there a number of possible treatments, any disease a Bichon might acquire can be treated with a variety of therapies," Dr. Messonnier says, "For example, small bladder stones might be dissolved with herbs. If this didn't work, surgery can be done, then followed up with supplements and a

Check with a holistic vet to see if complementary therapies might help treat your Bichon's conditions.

proper diet to minimise recurrence of the stones."

Check with a holistic vet to see if complementary therapies might help treat your Bichon's conditions.

FIRST AID AND OTHER EMERGENCIES

Sometimes a dog may have an accident or become ill, and you may need to provide first aid treatment before you contact your vet. Owners must recognise when emergency care is needed and be able to make the dog as comfortable as possible before receiving veterinary attention. Below are descriptions of signs and conditions that require immediate medical treatment, along with first aid techniques to use at home or on the way to the vet's.

Anaphylactic Shock

Allergic reactions can cause anaphylactic shock, a possibly fatal collapse of the body's systems. Reactions to drugs, insect bites, and some foods can result in hives, vomiting, difficulty breathing, swelling of airways, and shock. If your dog is conscious, you can give Benadryl (based on your vet's recommendation), and rush him to the surgery.

Bleeding (Uncontrolled)

Signs of uncontrolled bleeding include a copious flow of blood. Arterial blood is bright and spurts; blood from veins is dark and flows.
- Place sterile gauze (or clean cotton cloths if gauze is unavailable) over the wound and apply pressure.
- Tape the gauze in place for transport to the vet.
- Watch for swelling in the area below the bandage and slightly loosen the bandage to relieve it.

More severe bleeding may require the application of a tourniquet:
- Place a thick gauze pad over the wound.
- Wrap several layers of gauze or cloth around the gauze padding.
- Loop gauze tightly, insert a stick into the top of the loop and twist.
- Loosen the stick for 5 to 10 seconds every 10 to 15 minutes.

Broken Bones or Spinal Injury

Stabilise the break to limit movement and further damage.

- Temporarily splint the limb by wrapping loosely in multiple layers of gauze or newspaper.
- Carefully slide the dog on to a wooden plank or heavy cardboard, or wrap him in a heavy coat and transport to the vet for treatment. The dog may need to be muzzled, if it does not interfere with his breathing.

Burns

Burns are usually uncommon in dogs. But if it does happen to your Bichon, rinse with cool water and call your vet for further instructions. For severe or chemical burns, get immediate treatment.

First Aid Kit and Supplies

- Gauze pads, rolled gauze, first aid tape, rolled cotton-wool, cotton-wool balls, anti-bacterial wipes, self-clinging or vet wrap
- Hydrogen peroxide, antibiotic ointment, rubbing alcohol, petroleum jelly, sterile saline
- Pepto-Bismol or Kaopectate (NOTE: ingredients now contain salicylates, an aspirin-like substance that can exacerbate bleeding problems, gastrointestinal inflammation, or to which some dogs may be sensitive. It may also cause an adverse effect if given with certain other medications), Milk of Magnesia, Benadryl, Rescue Remedy, activated charcoal caps
- Scissors, tweezers, bulb syringe for administering medications, rectal thermometer
- Paper towels, towel, blanket, hot-cold pack, muzzle

Difficulty Breathing or Cardiovascular Distress

Signs include gasping, choking, straining to breathe, noise when breathing, rapid or shallow breathing, extreme anxiety, and collapse. As in human first aid, remember "ABC": airway, breathing, and circulation. Chest compressions or artificial respiration may be needed.

To perform chest compressions and artificial respiration:

- Open the dog's mouth, clear saliva, and remove any foreign objects if possible.
- Put the dog on his right side and place both hands on his chest; press down with a sharp motion and quickly release. Bichons are small, so be careful not to crack a rib. If the dog doesn't begin breathing, start artificial respiration.
- Hold the mouth tightly closed with your hand.
- Put your mouth over his nose, covering his nostrils, and blow gently for two to three seconds. The chest should expand if the airway is unobstructed.
- Continue respirations until the dog begins to breathe on his own.
- If loss of respiration is due to drowning, hold the dog upside down so water runs out. His head should be

positioned lower than his body.

If the heart is not beating, or no pulse can be felt, heart massage may be necessary. The dog should be in same position as for compressions and have his airway cleared. To perform heart massage:

- Put a thumb on one side and two fingers on other side of breastbone, behind the elbows.
- Compress six times, wait 5 seconds, and repeat. Repetitions may be continued until dog breathes or until no heartbeat is detected for 5 minutes.

Distended or Acute Abdomen

Signs include bloating with lack of gastrointestinal activity or sudden abdominal pain with retching and vomiting, restlessness, and assumption of a position with the chest down and abdomen up.

Possible causes are urinary stones, ruptured bladder, pancreatitis, bloat or torsion, intestinal obstruction. You must rush your dog to the vet—all conditions are life-threatening. Bloody or violent vomiting or diarrhoea also requires immediate treatment.

Eye Injury

Flush the eye with sterile saline, cover it with a sterile pad if drainage or bleeding is moderate to profuse, and get the dog to the vet.

Heatstroke

Exposure to hot temperatures for too long can cause fatal heatstroke. Signs are intensely rapid, raspy breathing, very red gums and tongue, thick saliva, moderate to severely elevated body temperature, and vomiting. Progression to death is rapid.

- Move the dog to a cool room or area, immerse in cool water, or spray him with a garden hose. If collapse is imminent, give a cool water enema.
- Veterinary treatment may include drugs to reduce heat-related inflammation.

Heatstroke is preventable; avoid situations where your dog could get overly warm. It only takes a few minutes for an unventilated vehicle, particularly if it's parked in direct sunlight, to exceed temperatures compatible with life.

Pet First Aid Training

Every responsible dog owner should master the principles of first aid so they can offer immediate help in an emergency situation.

Hypothermia

Exposure to cold temperatures for prolonged periods can result in hypothermia, which is the loss of minimum body temperature necessary to maintain life. Toy-sized dogs are most susceptible. Signs are violent shivering, apathy and lethargy, and a body temperature below 97°F (36°C).

- Move your dog to a warm room or area. Wrap him in towels or blankets.
- Warm water bottles can be applied over the towels. Hair dryers on a warm setting may also help, but monitor the dog during use of heating pads or dryers.
- When your dog is warm, give food to return his blood sugar (glucose) to normal levels.

Inability to Urinate

Signs include straining to urinate, no urine produced, or small amounts of bloody urine. Seek immediate treatment; your dog may need to be catheterised. Failure to pass urine can lead to kidney failure and death.

Neurological Symptoms

Signs include staggering gait, tremors, seizures, loss of balance, loss of consciousness, sudden loss of vision, and tilted head, sometimes with circling. Keep the dog calm and warm. Wrap him in a blanket to prevent self-injury and get medical attention.

Poison

Bichons, and Bichon puppies in particular, are inquisitive little animals and cannot resist investigating anything new they come across. Unfortunately, many substances and plants cause violent illness or death. Symptoms vary with the chemical ingested but include vomiting, diarrhoea, panting, drooling, salivating, difficulty breathing, seizures, loss of bladder or bowel control, coma, and death.

- Immediately try to locate the plant or substance ingested.
- Do not induce vomiting unless you are certain that it is appropriate; some agents are treated without inducing vomiting but are diluted with milk instead. Do not induce vomiting if the dog is unconscious or having seizures.

Car Dangers

Temperatures inside cars can rise dramatically even on mild days. With outside temperatures as low as 72°F (22°C), researchers have found that a car's interior temperature can heat up by an average of 40 degrees within an hour, with 80 percent of that increase in the first 30 minutes. A cracked window provides little relief from this oven effect.

- If induction of vomiting is advised, give 1 teaspoon hydrogen peroxide per 5 pounds of weight, to a maximum of 3 tablespoons. Activated charcoal may also be given, if advised, to help absorb some poisons.
- As soon as you have done as instructed, seek emergency treatment—be sure to bring the poison container with you; poisons may have long-lasting effects.

Shock

Shock can be the possible result of severe, acute trauma, allergy, or illness. It is detected by pale gums, shallow respiration, rapid heart rate, weakness or collapse, depression, confusion, and faint pulse.

- Check airway and breathing, and treat as described under *Trauma*, and control bleeding if applicable.
- Calm the dog and keep him warm.
- Do not impede his breathing by using a muzzle.
- Rush him to the vet without delay.

Remaning calm is the most important thing you can do for your Bichon in an emergency.

Trauma

If your Bichon suffers an accident or trauma due to a fall, if he is struck by a car, has a penetrating wound, a chest or abdominal wound, broken bones, severe bleeding or a neck, head, or back injury, shock may ensue. Muzzle the dog (unless he is having difficulty breathing), give first aid, and go for immediate treatment from your veterinary surgeon.

Muzzle Options

If you don't have a muzzle, gauze or strips of any soft cloth such as cotton rags or even a loose, cloth-covered elastic hair band may be substituted in an emergency.

THE VETERAN BICHON

As your Bichon ages, changes will occur in his health, such as difficulty moving, chewing, seeing, or hearing. It's hard to imagine when a dog is a cute puppy bouncing around, but growing old is inevitable. Providing appropriate support and care can allow your elderly Bichon to live a more comfortable life.

Physically, it is important to monitor his weight and nutrition. Health conditions common to older dogs can be made worse by obesity. Foods designed for veteran dogs provide the necessary nutrients in the proper amounts with fewer calories, thus reducing the chance of excess weight gain. Older dogs can also become too thin and may require a more appealing food that is higher in calories to maintain proper weight and energy level.

Although you may need to use gentler methods, don't stop grooming. Keep your Bichon bathed, brushed, and mat-free. Grooming improves skin and coat conditions that decline with age. And keep brushing your dog's teeth—bacteria from gum disease can put an extra strain on ageing organs.

Keep your older Bichon's space comfortable and healthy. Use soft, supportive bedding in a room that isn't cold, drafty, damp, or hot. Make sure water bowls are placed throughout the house so that he doesn't have to walk too far to get a drink. However, don't stop exercising your dog because he's older—activity promotes better circulation and digestion, which can be slowed in older dogs. Just don't overdo the exercise; plan activities around his limitations.

It's also a good idea to take the elderly Bichon to the vet for a check up twice a year as he ages. This provides an opportunity to catch age-related problems as they occur.

Ageing also effects emotional health. Changes in the brain can manifest as altered sleep–wake patterns, disorientation, or changes in behaviour. Canine nutritionists have found that antioxidants may be beneficial for the veteran dog's mental health. Additionally, keeping your older Bichon's mind stimulated has also been shown to help. This can be done by providing new toys, taking him for visits to play with other dogs, and interacting with people.

Probably the most important part of keeping the older Bichon healthy is to make him happy and to love him as much in his old age as you did when he was a puppy

Online Help

The Society of Companion Animal Studies (SCAS) provides a service where people can talk to a pet loss counsellor. Visit their website at www.scas.org.uk.

SAYING GOODBYE

A trite, old cliché says that all good things must come to an end. Sadly, this is true even for the life of a beloved dog. No matter when it occurs—at the end of a long life or following an early death from accident or disease—it will be too soon.

At that time, you may be called upon to make what may be the most difficult decision you will ever face: whether or not to euthanise your best friend.

Euthanisation is done as humanely as possible, by giving an overdose injection of a strong sedative. If your dog is anxious, a dose of a milder tranquiliser may be given prior to calm him. Most dogs simply lie down and close their eyes. A few may vocalise or experience mild twitching, but for the most part, their passing appears peaceful.

It is heart-wrenching to decide to end your dog's life, but it is equally painful to watch him lose his dignity, or die suffering or in pain. If you are having trouble making this decision, talk to your vet who will advise you what is best for your beloved Bichon.

As strange as it may be to believe, it is likely your dog will let you know when he is ready to let go. It may even be clear to you that he is asking you to help him be released. Or, your Bichon may die quietly in his sleep.

However your dog's death occurs, you may experience doubts about your actions and choices. You will also grieve over your loss. These feelings are normal, but you don't have to suffer in silence. There are a number of organisations that provide befriender services so that you can talk to a pet loss counsellor. For more information visit www.scas.org.uk or www.petloss.com.

Your days spent in each other's company may be over, but you will be left with your memories, so the best way to prepare for the eventual loss of your Bichon is to make the most of your time together now. Live your life with your canine companion in such a way that you have few regrets. Treat him well, take good care of him, play with him, travel with him, and love him. Then, when the day arrives that you say your final goodbyes, your memories will be that much sweeter, as the bond you shared lives on in your heart.

With care and love, your Bichon can be your best friend for years to come.

KENNEL CLUB BREED STANDARD

General Appearance: Well balanced dog of smart appearance, closely coated with handsome plume carried over the back. Natural white coat curling loosely. Head carriage proud and high.

Characteristics: Gay, happy, lively little dog.

Head and Skull: Ratio of muzzle length to skull length 3 : 5. On a head of the correct width and length, lines drawn between the outer corners of the eyes and nose will create a near equilateral triangle. Whole head in balance with body. Muzzle not thick, heavy nor snipey. Cheeks flat, not very strongly muscled. Stop moderate but definite, hollow between eyebrows just visible. Skull slightly rounded, not coarse, with hair accentuating rounded appearance. Nose large, round, black, soft and shiny.

Eyes: Dark, round with black eye rims, surrounded by dark haloes, consisting of well pigmented skin. Forward-looking, fairly large but not almond-shaped, neither obliquely set nor protruding. Showing no white when looking forward. Alert, full of expression.

Ears: Hanging close to head, well covered with flowing hair longer than leathers, set on slightly higher than eye level and rather forward on skull. Carried forward when dog alert, forward edge touching skull. Leather reaching approximately half-way along muzzle.

Mouth: Jaws strong, with a perfect, regular and complete scissor bite, i.e. upper teeth closely overlapping lower teeth and set square to the jaws. Full dentition desirable. Lips fine, fairly tight and completely black.

Neck: Arched neck fairly long, about one-third the length of body. Carried high and proudly. Round and slim near head, gradually broadening to fit smoothly into shoulders.

Forequarters: Shoulders oblique, not prominent, equal in length to upper arm. Upper arm fits close to body. Legs straight, perpendicular, when seen from front; not too finely boned. Pasterns short and straight viewed from front, very slightly sloping viewed from side.

Body: Forechest well developed, deep brisket. Ribs well sprung, floating ribs not terminating abruptly. Loin broad, well muscled, slightly arched and well tucked up. Pelvis broad, croup slightly rounded. Length from withers to tailset should equal height from withers to ground.

Hindquarters: Thighs broad and well rounded. Stifles well bent; hocks well angulated and metatarsals perpendicular.

Feet: Tight, rounded and well knuckled up. Pads black. Nails preferably black.

Tail: Normally carried raised and curved gracefully over the back but not tightly curled. Never docked. Carried in line with backbone, only hair touching back; tail itself not in contact. Set on level with topline, neither too high nor too low. Corkscrew tail undesirable.

Gait/Movement: Balanced and effortless with an easy reach and drive maintaining a steady and level topline. Legs moving straight along line of travel, with hind pads showing.

Coat: Fine, silky with soft corkscrew curls. Neither flat nor corded, and measuring 7-10 cms (3-4 ins) in length. The dog may be presented untrimmed or have muzzle and feet slightly tidied up.

Colour: White, but cream or apricot markings acceptable up to 18 months. Under white coat, dark pigment desirable. Black, blue or beige markings often found on skin.

Size: Ideal height 23-28 cms (9-11 ins) at withers.

Faults: Any departure from the foregoing points should be considered a fault and the seriousness with which the fault should be regarded should be in exact proportion to its degree and its effect upon the health and welfare of the dog.

Note: Male animals should have two apparently normal testicles fully descended into the scrotum.

March 1994

APPENDIX A

AKC BICHON FRISE BREED STANDARD

General Appearance: The Bichon Frise is a small, sturdy, white powder puff of a dog whose merry temperament is evidenced by his plumed tail carried jauntily over the back and his dark-eyed inquisitive expression.

This is a breed that has no gross or incapacitating exaggerations and therefore there is no inherent reason for lack of balance or unsound movement.

Any deviation from the ideal described in the standard should be penalized to the extent of the deviation. Structural faults common to all breeds are as undesirable in the Bichon Frise as in any other breed, even though such faults may not be specifically mentioned in the standard.

Size, Proportion, Substance: *Size* Dogs and bitches 9½ to 11½ inches are to be given primary preference. Only where the comparative superiority of a specimen outside this range clearly justifies it should greater latitude be taken. In no case, however, should this latitude ever extend over 12 inches or under 9 inches. The minimum limits do not apply to puppies. *Proportion*--The body from the forward-most point of the chest to the point of rump is ¼ longer than the height at the withers. The body from the withers to lowest point of chest represents ½ the distance from withers to ground. *Substance*--Compact and of medium bone throughout; neither coarse nor fine.

Head: *Expression*--Soft, dark-eyed, inquisitive, alert. *Eyes* are round, black or dark brown and are set in the skull to look directly forward. An overly large or bulging eye is a fault as is an almond shaped, obliquely set eye. Halos, the black or very dark brown skin surrounding the eyes, are necessary as they accentuate the eye and enhance expression. The eye rims themselves must be black. Broken pigment, or total absence of pigment on the eye rims produce a blank and staring expression, which is a definite fault. Eyes of any color other than black or dark brown are a very serious fault and must be severely penalized. *Ears* are drop and are covered with long flowing hair. When extended toward the nose, the leathers reach approximately halfway the length of the muzzle. They are set on slightly higher than eye level and rather forward on the skull, so that when the dog is alert they serve to frame the face. The *skull* is slightly rounded, allowing for a round and forward looking eye. The *stop* is slightly accentuated. *Muzzle*--A properly balanced head is three parts muzzle to five parts skull, measured from the nose to the stop and from the stop to the occiput. A line drawn between the outside corners of the eyes and to the nose will create a near equilateral triangle. There is a slight degree of chiseling under the eyes, but not so much as to result in a weak or snipey foreface. The lower jaw is strong. The *nose* is prominent and always black. *Lips* are black, fine, never drooping. *Bite* is scissors. A bite which is undershot or overshot should be severely penalized. A crooked or out of line tooth is permissible, however, missing teeth are to be severely faulted.

Neck, Topline and Body: The arched *neck* is long and carried proudly behind an erect head. It blends smoothly into the shoulders. The length of neck from occiput to withers is approximately 1/3 the distance from forechest to buttocks. The *topline* is level except for a slight, muscular arch over the loin. *Body*--The chest is well developed and wide enough to allow free and unrestricted movement of the front legs. The lowest point of the chest extends at least to the elbow. The rib cage is moderately sprung and extends back to a short and muscular loin. The forechest is well pronounced and protrudes slightly forward of the point of shoulder. The underline has a moderate tuck-up. *Tail* is well plumed, set on level with the topline and curved gracefully over the back so that the hair of the tail rests on the back. When the tail is extended toward the head it reaches at least halfway to the withers.

A low tail set, a tail carried perpendicularly to the back, or a tail which droops behind is to be severely penalized. A corkscrew tail is a very serious fault.

Forequarters: *Shoulders*--The shoulder blade, upper arm and forearm are approximately equal in length. The shoulders are laid back to somewhat near a forty-five degree angle. The upper arm extends well back so the elbow is placed directly below the withers when viewed from the side. **Legs** are of medium bone; straight, with no bow or curve in the forearm or wrist. The elbows are held close to the body. The *pasterns* slope slightly from the vertical. The dewclaws may be removed. The *feet* are tight and round, resembling those of a cat and point directly forward, turning neither in nor out. *Pads* are black. **Nails** are kept short.

Hindquarters: The hindquarters are of medium bone, well angulated with muscular thighs and spaced moderately wide. The upper and lower thigh are nearly equal in length meeting at a well bent stifle joint. The leg from hock joint to foot pad is perpendicular to the ground. Dewclaws may be removed. Paws are tight and round with black pads.

Coat: The texture of the coat is of utmost importance. The undercoat is soft and dense, the outercoat of a coarser and curlier texture. The combination of the two gives a soft but substantial feel to the touch which is similar to plush or velvet and when patted springs back. When bathed and brushed, it stands off the body, creating an overall powder puff appearance. A wiry coat is not desirable. A limp, silky coat, a coat that lies down, or a lack of undercoat are very serious faults. *Trimming*--The coat is trimmed to reveal the natural outline of the body. It is rounded off from any direction and never cut so short as to create an overly trimmed or squared off appearance. The furnishings of the head, beard, moustache, ears and tail are left longer. The longer head hair is trimmed to create an overall rounded impression. The topline is trimmed to appear level. The coat is long enough to maintain the powder puff look which is characteristic of the breed.

Color: Color is white, may have shadings of buff, cream or apricot around the ears or on the body. Any color in excess of 10% of the entire coat of a mature specimen is a fault and should be penalized, but color of the accepted shadings should not be faulted in puppies.

Gait: Movement at a trot is free, precise and effortless. In profile the forelegs and hind legs extend equally with an easy reach and drive that maintain a steady topline. When moving, the head and neck remain somewhat erect and as speed increases there is a very slight convergence of legs toward the center line. Moving away, the hindquarters travel with moderate width between them and the foot pads can be seen. Coming and going, his movement is precise and true.

Temperament: Gentle mannered, sensitive, playful and affectionate. A cheerful attitude is the hallmark of the breed and one should settle for nothing less.

Approved October 11, 1988
Effective November 30, 1988

WHAT TO DO WHEN IT DOESN'T WORK OUT

If you've done your homework, picked what you thought was the perfect breed and just the right Bichon for your home, then chances are you and your dog will live happily ever after. But what should you do if the relationship with your dog isn't as happy as a fairy tale?

First, realise that not every day with a dog will be a good one. You should learn to take the good with the bad. However, if you *and* the dog are constantly unhappy, the relationship may not be working, despite your best efforts.

Before you give up:

- Have your dog thoroughly examined by a vet. Some behaviour problems are caused by medical issues, many of which can be treated;
- Consult with a behaviourist or training consultant who may be able to correct problematic behaviour;
- Take your Bichon to a training class;
- Examine your lifestyle—can it be changed to adapt to your dog's needs? Can your dog's exercise or nutrition be changed to help cope with a problem?

If these steps don't resolve the problem, some signs that may indicate your dog might be better off in a different home include:

- A drastic change in your life that has rendered you incapable of caring for your dog on a long-term basis, either financially, physically or emotionally;
- An inability to provide needed medical care on a regular basis;
- A lack of time or finances to groom your Bichon, and his coat is seriously matted most of the time;
- Your dog is often alone or is crated or confined most of the time, is depressed and losing interest in his surroundings;
- You have become uninterested in your dog or his welfare;
- You are emotionally unable to cope with your dog's problems and have relegated him to the garden, or to one room, or you have resorted to using physical punishment on your dog.

If it becomes necessary to rehome your dog:

- Contact your breeder first about taking the dog back, this is the preferred option;
- Locate the closest Bichon rescue group and ask them to take in your dog for adoption into a new home;
- Provide the rescue group with a thorough and honest history of your dog's health and behaviour, which will give him the best chance of getting a good home.
- Do not sell or give your dog away to strangers that may not be qualified to care for him.
- If you need to take your Bichon to a rehoming centre, check that it has a "no destruct" policy, so you can be sure your dog will be rehomed.

APPENDIX B

RESOURCES

ASSOCIATIONS AND ORGANISATIONS

BREED CLUBS AND KENNEL CLUBS

Bichon Frisé Club of Great Britain
Hon.Secretary - Mrs D. Russell, 129 The Diplocks, Hailsham, East Sussex, BN27 3JY
Tel: 01323 843947
E-mail: dawn@rusmar.fsnet.co.uk
www.bichonfriseclubofgb.info

Bichon Frise Club of America
32 Oak Street
Centreeach, NY, 11720
Corresponding Secretary:
Joanne Styles
Telephone: 631 588 2250
www.bichon.org

Bichon Frise Club of Canada
Secretary: Marilyn Torrance
E-mail: bichons@istar.ca

American Kennel Club (AKC)
5580 Centreview Drive
Raleigh, NC 27606
Telephone: 919 233 9767
Fax: 919 233 3627
E-mail: info@akc.org
www.akc.org

Canadian Kennel Club (CKC)
89 Skyway Avenue, Suite 100
Etobicoke, Ontario M9W 6R4
Telephone: 416 675 5511
Fax: 416 675 6506
E-mail: information@ckc.ca
www.ckc.ca

Federation Cynologique Internationale (FCI)
Secretariat General de la FCI
Place Albert 1er, 13
B – 6530 Thuin
Belqique
www.fci.be

The Kennel Club
1 Clarges Street
London
W1J 8AB
Telephone: 0870 606 6750
Fax: 0207 518 1058
www.the-kennel-club.org.uk

United Kennel Club (UKC)
100 E. Kilgore Road
Kalamazoo, MI 49002-5584
Telephone: 269 343 9020
Fax: 269 343 7037
E-mail: pbickell@ukcdogs.com
www.ukcdogs.com

PET SITTERS

National Association of Registered Petsitters
www.dogsit.com

UK Petsitters
Telephone: 01902 41789
www.ukpetsitter.com

Dog Services UK
www.dogservices.co.uk

RESCUE ORGANIZATIONS AND ANIMAL WELFARE GROUPS

British Veterinary Association Animal Welfare Foundation (BVA AWF)
7 Mansfield Street
London W1G 9NQ
Telephone: 0207 636 6541
Fax: 0207 436 2970
Email: bva-awf@bva.co.uk
www.bva-awf.org.uk/about

Royal Society for the Prevention of Cruelty to Animals (RSPCA)
Telephone: 0870 3335 999
Fax: 0870 7530 284
www.rspca.org.uk

Scottish Society for the Prevention of Cruelty to Animals (SSPCA)
Braehead Mains
603 Queensferry Road
Edinburgh EH4 6EA
Telephone: 0131 339 0222
Fax: 0131 339 4777

Email: enquiries@
scottishspca.org
www.scottishspca.org/about

SPORTS

Agility Club UK
www.agilityclub.co.uk

British Flyball Association
PO Box 109
Petersfield GU32 1XZ
Telephone: 01753 620110
Fax: 01726 861079
Email: bfa@flyball.org.uk
www.flyball.org.uk

**Canine Freestyle
Federation, Inc.**
Secretary: Brandy Clymire
E-Mail: secretary@canine-
freestyle.org
www.canine-freestyle.org

**International Agility Link
(IAL)**
Global Administrator: Steve
Drinkwater
E-mail: yunde@powerup.au
www.agilityclick.com/~ial

**World Canine Freestyle
Organisation**
P.O. Box 350122
Brooklyn, NY 11235-2525
Telephone: (718) 332-8336
www.worldcaninefreestyle.
org

THERAPY

Pets As Therapy
3 Grange Farm Cottages
Wycombe Road, Saunderton
Princes Risborough
Bucks HP27 9NS
Telephone: 0870 977 0003
Fax: 0870 706 2562
www.petsastherapy.org

**Therapy Dogs International
(TDI)**
88 Bartley Road
Flanders, NJ 07836
Telephone: (973) 252-9800
Fax: (973) 252-7171
E-mail: tdi@gti.net
www.tdi-dog.org

TRAINING

**Association of Pet Dog
Trainers (APDT)**
PO Box 17
Kempsford GL7 4W7
Telephone: 01285 810811

**Association of Pet
Behaviour Counsellors**
PO Box 46
Worcester WR8 9YS
Telephone: 01386 751151
Fax: 01386 750743
Email: info@apbc.org.uk
www.apbc.org.uk

VETERINARY AND HEALTH RESOURCES

**Association of British
Veterinary Acupuncturists
(ABVA)**
66A Easthorpe
Southwell
Nottinghamshire NG25 0HZ
Email: jonnyboyvet@
hotmail.com
www.abva.co.uk

**Association of Chartered
Physiotherapists
Specialising in Animal
Therapy (ACPAT)**
52 Littleham Road
Exmoouth, Devon EX8 2QJ
Telephone/Fax: 01395
270648
Email: bexsharples@hotmail.
com
www.acpat.org.uk

**British Association of
Homoeopathic Veterinary
Surgeons**
Alternative Veterinary
Medicine Centre
Chinham House
Stanford in the Vale
Oxfordshire SN7 8NQ
Email: enquiries@bahvs.com
www.bahvs.com

**British Association of
Veterinary Opthalmologists
(BAVO)**
Email: hjf@vetspecialists.
co.uk
Email: secretary@bravo.org.
uk
www.bravo.org.uk

British Small Animal Veterinary Association (BSAVA)
Woodrow House
1 Telford Way
Waterwells Business Park
Quedgley
Gloucester GL2 2AB
Telephone: 01452 726700
Fax: 01452 726701
Email: customerservices@bsava.com
www.bsava.com

British Veterinary Hospitals Association (BHVA)
Station Bungalow
Main Road, Stockfield
Northumberland NE43 7HJ
Telephone: 07966 901619
Fax: 07813 915954
Email: office@bvha.org.uk
www.BVHA.org.uk

Royal College of Veterinary Surgeons (RCVS)
Belgravia House
62-64 Horseferry Road
London SW1P 2AF
Telephone: 0207 222 2001
Fax: 0207 222 2004
Email: admin@rcvs.org.uk
www.rcvs.org.uk

British Veterinary Association (BVA)
7 Mansfield Street
London
W1G 9NQ
Telephone: 020 7636 6541
Fax: 020 7436 2970
E-mail: bvahq@bva.co.uk
www.bva.co.uk

American Veterinary Medical Association (AVMA)
1931 North Meacham Road – Suite 100
Schaumburg, IL 60173
Telephone: (847) 925-8070
Fax: (847) 925-1329
E-mail: avmainfo@avma.org
www.avma.org

PUBLICATIONS

BOOKS

Barnes, Julia
Living With a Rescued Dog
Dorking: Interpet Publishing, 2004

Evans, J M & White, Kay
Doglopaedia
Dorking: Ringpress, 1998

Evans, J M
Book of The Bitch
Dorking: Ringpress, 1998

Tennant, Colin
Mini Encyclopedia of Dog Training & Behaviour
Dorking: Interpet Publishing, 2005

Evans, J M
What If my Dog?
Dorking: Interpet Publishing, 2005

NEWSPAPERS & MAGAZINES

Dog World Ltd
Somerfield House
Wotton Road, Ashford
Kent TN23 6LW
Telephone: 01233 621877
Fax: 01233 645669

Dogs Monthly
Ascot House
High Street, Ascot,
Berkshire SL5 7JG
United Kingdom
Telephone: 0870 730 8433
Fax: 0870 730 8431
E-mail: admin@rtc-associates.freeserve.co.uk
www.corsini.co.uk/dogsmonthly

Dogs Today
Town Mill, Bagshot Road
Chobham
Surrey GU24 8BZ
Telephone: 01276 858880
Fax: 01276 858860
Email: enquiries@dogstoday magazine.co.uk
www.dogstodaymagazine.co.uk

Kennel Gazette
Kennel Club
1 Clarges Street
London W1J 8AB
Telephone: 0870 606 6750
Fax: 0207 518 1058
www.the-kennel-club.co.uk

K9 Magazine
21 High Street
Warsop
Nottinghamshire NG20
0AA
Telephone: 0870 011 4114
Fax: 0870 706 4564
Email: mail@k9magazine.
com
www.k9magazine.com

Our Dogs
Our Dogs Publishing
5 Oxford Road
Station Approach
Manchester M60 1SX
www.ourdogs.co.uk

Your Dog
Roebuck House
33 Broad Street
Stamford
Lincolnshire PE9 1RB
Telephone: 01780 766199
Fax: 01780 766416

WEBSITES

BichonFrise-L
UK:www.bflmembers.co.uk/
index.htm
US: www.bichonfrise.org/
bfl/bichon.html
Internet e-mail discussion
list.

Bichon Information
www.bichons.btinternet.
co.uk

Pages of information all
about Bichons.

Bichon Rescue
www.bichonfriserescue.
co.uk/
Bichon rescue in the United
Kingdom.

DEDICATION

To Libbet, who left me—much too soon—during the writing of this book. Each morning, you led us in a howling song of joy to greet and celebrate the new day. Godspeed Libbet. May you sing with the angels now.

ACKNOWLEDGEMENTS

I would like to extend a very big "thank you" to all the Bichon folks who provided input and insights for this book. Thanks go especially to the joyful one; the candy man; Buttons and Beau and your humom; the members, both public and private, of 0-A-Wee Bichon Lovers and Bichon Frise discussion lists; the veterinarians; the groomer extraordinaire; the trainers, breeders, competitors, rescue workers and owners, for sharing your time, knowledge, experience and dogs with me.

To the Bichons themselves, thank you for showing me your playful, loving nature. May the information in this book help bring about a world where no more Bichons ever need rescued.

ABOUT THE AUTHOR

Lexiann Grant is an internationally published, award-winning pet writer and photographer who has raised, trained, shown, written, and spoken about dogs and cats for many years. She is a professional member of the Dog Writers Association of America and has been a recipient of the Maxwell Medallion eight times. Ms. Grant works full-time in her home office, where much of her time is spent observing the pets with whom she lives. In addition to her life that revolves around animals, Ms. Grant cycles, skis, practices yoga, and is a chocolate addict. She and her husband reside in southeastern Ohio with three dogs, three cats, and four bicycles.

PHOTO CREDITS

Photo on page 10 courtesy of Tara Darling
Photo on page 49 courtesy of Vince Serbin
Photos on page 53, 59, 85, 87, 97, 103, 138, 141 (bottom), 144, 145 courtesy of Lexiann Grant
Photo on page 64 courtesy of Robert Pearcy
Photos on page 94, 95, 163, 167 courtesy of Anthony Delprete
All other photos courtesy of Isabelle Francais